For the weapons of our warfare are not carnal but are mighty through God to the pulling down of strongholds....

2 Corinthians 10: 4

And there is none that calls upon thy name, that wakes himself to take hold of thee.

Isaiah 64:7

'Yeah, they turned back and tempted God. They limited the Holy One of Israel.'

Psalms 78:41

'It seems that God is limited by our prayers.'

John Wesley

PREAMBLE

Oral Roberts and Kenneth E Hagin, two contemporaries, were in a deep conversation, when a stranger walked up to them and said 'I just want to shake hands with these great competitors.'

They were not competitors.

They were co-laborers in the vineyard of the Lord.

Although at face value their positions on seed -faith giving appeared to differ, their positions and experiences on new depths of prayer were startlingly similar. Kenneth E Hagin remarked that nobody he ever knew, knew how to enter into the presence of the Lord in prayer like Oral Roberts. Brother Hagin knew this because he had prayed with Oral Roberts at times. He too had been up there several times in prayer and feared that he might not come back. He thought he might not come back at times. Enoch went out so far in the spiritual realm he did not come back –KEH observed.

When Kenneth E Hagin and Oral Roberts compared notes they discovered that the pattern of their ministries had been unveiled to them in exactly the same way: speaking in tongues and interpreting them. This had given the direction/trajectory their ministries took over the years. These principles apply to one's career, studies, business pursuits, marital life and what have you! As we avail ourselves to the Lord, going deeper and deeper in praying in tongues, the Lord will lead us into a deeper realm of prayer where miracles and revelations abound.

Kenneth E Hagin (KEH) noted how several decades ago, America became concerned when the Russians were able to put the first Sputnik out in space. Billions of dollars were poured into the space race. However the early astronauts didn't go far. They only barely left the earth's atmosphere: they didn't know how to maneuver in space. In the same manner, observes KEH, some of us have reached the 'edge of the Spirit Realm in prayer.' We however don't know how to maneuver out there and therefore as prayer warriors we need to know how to press into new depths of prayer.

When more and more saints pray, the manifestation of the presence of God, and the demonstration of the Holy Ghost will be commonplace! It will be the rule and not the exception. We have been like children wading in water, at the edge of the body of water, saying 'O what a great experience we have had.' There is a deeper experience to have. Many have only touched the edge realm of the spirit at a tangent but have not been fully immersed in it. We need to go further than knee deep, loin deep and swim in the Spirit as the Prophet Ezekiel did in the book of Ezekiel 47. There is a call to the body of Christ to wait upon the Lord. 'Flow in the gifts of the Holy Spirit.' Kenneth E Hagin would urge.

At one point KEH attended an 'Idea Exchange,' meeting. Many Ministers from various denominations attended. Some of the ministers approached KEH and asked him,

'When I first knew you, nobody had ever heard of you. You were preaching in small churches and, once in a while, in a large church. But then, all of a sudden, you became not only a national figure, but in just a matter of years – an international figure.......what is your secret of success?'

KEH answered,

'The only secret of success I know is walking in line with the word of God, and praying and listening to the Holy Spirit.'

He said 'Actually everything I am doing today is the result of believing the word, praying in tongues and being obedient to what God has told me to do.'

Like Oral Roberts he would say 'thank God for the value of praying in tongues....praying in tongues was instrumental in even [God] showing me about my marriage and my children.'

Folks there are greater depths of prayer we ought to press into. KEH exhorted the saints to spend more time in the things of God. Other things maybe legitimate, but they must not get in the way of the things of the Spirit.

Do you want to move into greater depths of prayer?. Do you want to flow into deeper dimensions of prayer, the summit of a prayer life where miracles abound? This holy Ghost sanctioned book is sent to propel the saint into becoming a mighty prayer champion who moves mountains, moves in the realm of the miraculous and knows no biding impossibilities: just boundless possibilities. Here, the anatomy of praying in the power of the Spirit is explored as gleaned from the granary of mighty men of God who did exploits. We can become mighty in prayer, birthing souls into the kingdom, experience explosive church growth, breathtaking breakthroughs in our ministries, careers, business pursuits, studies, marital life and -----O folks the list is interminable!

Now to him who is able to [carry out his purpose and] do superabundantly more than all that we dare ask or think [infinately beyond prayers, hopes or dreams,] according to the power that is at work in us.

Ephesians 3:20

2 Corithians 10:4 says

(For the weapons of our warfare are not carnal but are mighty through God to the pulling down of strongholds;)

CHAPTER ONE: Praying in the Spirit for the Unknown.

***Praying always with all prayer and supplication in the Spirit, and watching thereunto with all perseverance and supplication for all saints*.**

Ephesians 6: 18

Paul urges the Saints to pray in the Spirit. Benny Hinn once said 'you need to be in the realm of the spirit to get results.' It's not about prayer per se. People in every religion pray. It is about communion with the Lord in the power of the Holy Spirit. Some people think that praying in the Holy Ghost is praying with a little more vim, verve and gusto than usual. Yes, the Spirit lends fervency to our prayer life but there is a far deeper dimension than just that. A dimension that is both a mystery and supernatural. A dimension that gives ability. Power!

A look at Romans 8: 26, 27 throws light on the potency and indispensability of the Holy Ghost in prayer.

Romans 8

26. Likewise the Spirit also helpeth our infirmities: for we know not what to pray for as we ought but the Spirit itself maketh intercession for us with groaning[s] which cannot be uttered.

27. And he that searcheth the hearts knoweth what is the mind of the Spirit, because he maketh intercession for the saints according to the will of God.

Without the Holy Spirit we are lost in a mist of ignorance: 'for we know not what to pray for as we ought...'

We face a severe handicaps: there are hidden impediments in our life and elusive opportunities yet we don't really know what they are and the most effectual way to pray for them.

The Holy Spirit, by God's grace helpeth our infirmities. He offset the ignorance deficit.

Romans 8 vs.26

Likewise the Spirit also **helpeth** our infirmities.

In his book *Bodily Healing and The Atonement,* Dr McCrossan, looked at the etymology of the word suntantilambanetai, which is Greek for helpeth. He notes that 'Sun' means 'together with'; anti denotes 'against'; lambano denotes 'take hold together with.'

Dr McCrossan concludes that helpeth means 'to take hold together with against.'

Romans 8 vs. 26 therefore means that the Holy Spirit *helps us by taking hold together with us against* our infirmities. That's powerful! Kenneth E Hagin gives the analogy of moving a piano from a platform, down to the floor. One might ask others to help him move the piano. In essence one will actually be asking others to hold together with him against the weight of the piano. Similarly the Holy Spirit holds together with us against our weaknesses, shortcomings, limitations and all other ills.

The Holy Spirit in this new dispensation is our main helper.

John 14: 16-18; 26 says

'And I will pray the Father, and he shall give you another Comforter, that he might abide with you forever; Even the Spirit of truth; ----------I will not leave you comfortless----.

But the Comforter, which is the Holy Ghost, whom the Father will send in my name, he shall teach you all things, and bring all things to your remembrance, whatsoever I have said unto you.'

The term 'Comforter' in Greek is *Paraclete* which literally means 'one called alongside to help.'

So the Holy Spirit *is called alongside to help by holding together with us against* our infirmities! Glory Hallelujah. If you are not praying in the power of the Holy Ghost, who are you holding together with? Who are you holding together with against the challenges to your ministry, career, marriage, education and what have you?

What is one of the defining characteristic of 'our infirmities?' Here infirmities is used as a variant term for weakness or shortcomings. We don't know what to pray for as we ought and we don't know how to pray as we ought. Not knowing is our severe handicap, as pointed out earlier.

'for we know not what to pray for as we ought...'

O, we don't know what lies ahead. We don't know how to effectively pray for tomorrow. Mankind has a maddeningly limited capacity to anticipate evil. We don't fully know our tomorrow. We don't know the full extent of the opposing forces and we have a dimmed perception of the urgency of matters close to our heavenly Father. Thank God, the Holy Spirit knows these and he is called alongside to help! The Holy Spirit is called alongside to hold together with us against the adversity which might be outside our natural perception. We don't know the mind of the Lord in our present circumstances at times. We are likely to follow our instincts and not the Lord's bidding. Praying in the Holy Spirit enables us to clear this hurdle, again and again and again.

Unknown to us, Satan has made an enquiry over our marriages. Unknown to us Satan has an enquiry made about a specific member of the church. Not known to us, due to our infirmity of limited to non-existent insight and foresight at times, the enemy is salivating at the thought of your next challenge becoming your ultimate demise. He means to sift you as your wheat. He means to scatter us to the four winds. He wants our spiritual landscape stripped, bare and desolate. The hidden dangers are laid bare by the Lord as we pray in the power of the Holy Spirit.

How often we walk past doors which the Lord has opened because of our lack of spiritual perception. When we pray in the power of the Holy Ghost, our eyes are opened and we are led to the territories which we must take. We are led to win the souls which we are blind to. We are led to the church growth which remains elusive as we labour with our strength. Ecclesiastics 10:10 says

If you don't sharpen your ax, it will be harder to use; if you are wise you will know what to do.

Contemporary English Version.

It is the Holy Spirit who knows the best route to take to realise your potential. Without his direction it's all hit and miss and you must exert more strength. You will toil to no avail. May we pray in the power of the Holy Ghost-for by strength alone shall no man prevail.

Thank God for the Holy Ghost. The Holy Spirit is called alongside to hold with us against the danger to our marriage which is lurking in the shadows. The Holy Spirit is called alongside to hold with us against the enemy's evil devices against a church member whose full details may not be fully known to us. The Holy Spirit is called alongside to hold with us against the unknown obstacle he has thrown in our way to thwart our progress in the ministry, in career, business pursuits, and academic endeavours and so forth. It's a mystery to us. Yet as we pray in the power of the Holy Ghost, speaking mysteries to and with the Lord, the enemy comes undone, the path is made straight. O how untraceable is the path of the Lord.

The Goodwins Pray a Congregant Out of an Unknown Deadly Situation.

During the Second World War, Reverend Goodwin and his wife were the Pastors of an east Texas church. During the night, Mrs Goodwin had an urge to pray and was soon groaning deeply in the spirit. She tried hard to contain herself so as not wake her husband up. The groanings however got deeper and louder and disturbed her husband. She told her husband that she had a burden to pray: a church member was in grave danger. She could not tell who it was. Reverend Goodwin and his wife could only think of four families driving back in the night from a holiday. They prayed and claimed divine protection for the families. Brother Goodwin went back to sleep while his wife struggled to sleep. Still, the burden lingered. She started to groan again until she woke her husband up. She told him that they had prayed for the wrong party: it was someone else who was in danger. They went back to praying and prayed for hours on end in tongues. The sense of heaviness did not lift. Finally Reverend Goodwin told his wife that they should pray that whoever's life was in danger should have a vision from the Lord about the pending danger. This they did, and having some form of relief went to sleep. It was 4 am when they finally went to sleep. They were still fast asleep when the phone rang.

On the other end of the phone was one of their church members, the Sunday School Superintendent. The Sunday School Superintendent had quite a story to tell about what had just happened at work. He had turned up for work at one of the oil wells, where he worked. They worked in teams called 'gangs' those days. When he arrived for work that morning, he was asked to go up the ladder and work on the tower, by the gangmaster. Bill, the man who normally worked the tower was absent. The church member began to go up. He then changed his mind and came down, telling the baffled 'gang pusher' that he was not going to do it. *He had dreamt at **4 am** in the morning that Bill had not turned up for work and he had to replace him up the tower. He had gone up the tower, and a cable broke and cut his head off. He had actually seen his head fall on the ground. He was adamant: he was not going to go up the tower.* Someone else volunteered to go up, stating that he was not superstitious and did not believe that he will come to any harm. The volunteer went up. The cable came loose, cut his head off and the head fell down hitting the Sunday School Superintendent on the shoulder. This volunteer was a Christian who attended a church across the street from the Goodwins' church. ***Praying in the Holy Spirit, letting the Holy Spirit come alongside to help and hold with the Goodwins against the unknown danger made the difference between life and death***.

Yet another life and death scenario.

In 1956, the late Reverend Kenneth E Hagin (KEH) and his family held a meeting in California. They were traveling in a large trailer. One night while sound asleep KEH felt as if someone had nudged him in the ribs. Then he thought he heard the door slam. He looked around the trailer and saw nothing untoward. Everyone else was sound asleep. The doors were locked and windows closed. He wondered why he had been awakened like that.

In his own words, he began to put up his spiritual antenna- reach out with his spirit to the Almighty God for enlightenment. He felt in his spirit that one of his kinfolk was in danger. He couldn't tell who it was. He asked the Holy Spirit to help him. He started praying in tongues in the mould of Smith Wigglesworth who said,

'I began in the flesh and wound up in the spirit.'

He prayed for a considerable length of time without unction or anointing until the words started to just pour out of his mouth. 'I hit the gusher.' KEH would say in his home spun folksy style. All along he lay next to his sleeping wife and

never disturbed her.
He kept praying for more than an hour and a half until he knew he had 'prayed through.' How does one know that he has prayed through? He prays until he gets an assurance in his heart, a note of victory; laughter or singing in the spirit; a knowing in the heart and many other peculiar ways the Lord will use to deal with an individual. KEH began to sing quietly to himself and laugh in the spirit.

'Those old timers. They knew how to pray through.' KEH would enthuse.

Then a rare occurrence took place that night. He had a dream. He was in Shreveport, Louisiana and across the street was a hotel. His young brother Pat was staying there. Pat had given his life to the Lord but was not walking right before the Lord at that time.
In the dream KEH saw Pat taken sick. He was admitted as a matter of emergency after being rushed into the hospital by an ambulance. KEH saw himself standing outside the treatment room. He saw the Doctor come out and tell him, 'He is gone.'
KEH argued that Pat was alive: indeed the Lord Jesus had told him so.
To put the matter to rest, the Doctor ushered him into the treatment room and rolled back the sheet covering Pat.
'Look,' the Doctor said.
At that juncture, Pat blinked, much to the Doctor's amazement.
This was in May. In August KEH and family went back to their

home in Garland, Texas. They were taking the trailer back into the backyard when Pat came to the back to greet them. He started telling them about how he almost died while they were away. KEH interrupted him and told him exactly what happened in Shreveport. A wide eyed Pat wondered how his brother had come to know all this.
Thank God for the Holy Spirit!
KEH said he had countless experiences along those lines.

Praying Through.

It is important to reiterate the point of 'praying through.' The saint must not only drop to his knees, pray a bit and then jump back to his feet without getting a note of victory or the assurance in his heart that he has prevailed over the circumstances or the adversity. You need to have a knowing in your heart that you have had your breakthrough in the spiritual world. It will be a matter of time before the breakthrough manifests itself in the material world. Once you have the assurance, you stand on it and hold fast to your confession of victory and wait for your victory to be visible. That is how you walk in faith. Smith Wigglesworth said 'it is when we stand believing that there will be a performance.'

He also said,

'We stand believing and having done all, we still stand believing.'

Kenneth E Hagin had a missionary friend who had laboured in Africa during the First World War. Intercontinental

communication was not that great in Africa then.
The friend's wife Blanche had parents who were old time Pentecostals living off their deteriorating dairy farm.
One morning Blanche's father was coming from milking the remaining three cows when he suddenly had an inner impression that someone was in danger. He knew it was something to do with Blanche. The Farmer's wife was about to make breakfast when he burst into the house. She noticed that her husband looked like he had just seen a ghost. The old farmer urged his wife to join him in prayer: their daughter was in danger. Something inside him indeed told him thus.
They got down to prayer.
The old farmer told the Holy Spirit that they did not know what to pray for but were depending on him. They broke into tongues. This was at half five in the morning but they went on to pray for hours on end. At around two pm the Farmer began to laugh and sing in tongues. He suddenly proclaimed to his wife that Blanche was going to be alright.
KEH says 'now let me stress this one more time, once you begin to pray this way keep on praying until you get a note of victory.'
When you get an urge to laugh, sing or worship or simply a knowing and assurance in your heart, you must take that to mean you have prayed 'your burden through.'(Hagin 2007:304)

'Those old timers. They knew how to pray through.' KEH would enthuse. Billy Bryce used to be KEH's editor. Presently,

Billy Bryce's ministry is to help the 'Pray-ers.' KEH urged her to teach the younger generations to maintain the old timers' practice of 'praying through.'

Remember that Medical practices in Africa in those days were a bit on the primitive side. Blanche had been afflicted by a common deadly fever that was just as good as a death sentence. Her chances of survival were next to nothing. She miraculously recovered at some point. On corresponding with Blanche and her husband the old Farmer and his wife found that the times Blanche fell sick and recovered corresponded with that day's prayer timeline!

<u>Don't Quench the Holy Spirit.</u>

Praying for the unknown requires us to follow the leading of the Holy Spirit. The bible says the Holy Spirit shall lead us into all truth. Where he leads, we must follow. We must be spiritually sensitive to his bidding and direction. The following episode is instructive.

Upon marrying KEH and his young wife Oretha had nowhere to live since the Tom Bean church they were pastoring had no parsonage. He had been renting a room from one of the church members. His father –in-law had suggested that he comes and makes his abode with them in their large farmhouse, once he gets married. There was plenty of room there and it was going to give them a start in life as he wouldn't have to pay rent. KEH moved in four days after marriage. At 21:30 his mother -in-law invited everyone for a family prayer. KEH notes that they were Methodists. KEH asserts that they were attending the Full Gospel church when he came to pastor it, but they were not 'Pentecostal' as such. They all prayed out loud in English that night. The parents though were not very vocal, having come from a denominational background given to an excess account of solemnity. Their youthful son-in-law was trying to mind his decibels, a hard thing to do given that he kept having this red-hot urge to pray loudly in tongues. Won't the in laws be apprehensive about the tongues?

The urge to pray in tongues though kept intensifying, building and boiling inside him. Finally he burst out and lifted his voice and prayed out loud in tongues fast and hard. He shut his eyes, not wanting to catch his in-laws' eye, especially after raising their ire as he feared. After 45 minutes of prayer like that, the Lord spoke to him. He didn't know it was the Lord at first. Despite his precocious growth in the things of the Lord he still had a lot to learn and was ever keen to know and get the Lord God's best and more. He said that in Pentecostal circles those days, all they taught you was to give your life to the Lord, receive the baptism of the Holy Ghost and then 'turn you loose.' Whatever you were going to know, you had to 'stumble' upon it!

After the Lord bade him three times to lay his hands on her, he realized it was the voice of the Lord. He had never laid his hands on anyone before. He looked around with trepidation. His father-in law was on his right side; his young wife was on his left and his mother-in- law was kneeling on his wife's left side. The Lord, Brother Hagin was to say later on, will put up with some unbelief when you are grappling with a new issue but later on the Lord will demand more from you. Gingerly, he stretched his hands and laid them on top of her head. She had no 'instructions ---never sought baptism in the Holy Spirit all her life.' KEH observed.

She was filled! She prayed and sang in tongues for hours.

At around midnight, after they had prayed and sung in tongues, the Lord laid on his heart the need to pray for his mother –in –law to be healed. She had a double goiter. Her suitcase was already packed to go to the hospital. The spirit told him what to he ought to do for her to receive her healing. ***He did as he was told, and she was healed.*** She never had the operation. KEH noted that 'The part of the goiter on the outside went down like you had stuck a pin in a balloon.'

When he was praying out aloud and agonizing in tongues, he was actually interceding for both his wife and mother-in-law. It resulted in life changing experiences for both ladies. In intercession it is essential to be in the power of the Holy Spirit and be sensitive to his biddings. The Holy Spirit is called 'the comforter' -in Greek lexicon, as we have seen, that means 'one called along to help.' But how can two walk together until they agree? We must not quench the Holy Ghost.

The late Evangelist John Lake's daughter Gertrude talked about how praying in the spirit for someone or something can take you beyond what you initially set out to pray for. In one meeting in the US, a lady was lost in the spirit having started to intercede for her family. She spoke in tongues for a long time as the congregation basked in the glory of the Lord. Later on another woman of Croatian descent approached the praying lady who had prayed in tongues for a long time and thanked her. The woman revealed that the praying woman had not only prayed for her own American family in a Croatian dialect but she had interceded for the Croatian woman's family and mentioned the Croatian's family members' names, town streets and buildings back in Croatia!

'Talk about two in one!' Gertrude quipped.

CHAPTER TWO: TRAVAILIING FOR SOULS.

Oral Roberts stated that short prayers do it and long prayers do it as well. There are many types of prayer.

O how often a times, from many a platform we heard the late Reverend Kenneth Hagin quote Ephesians 6:18 which says

Pray at all times (on every occasion, in every season) in the spirit, with all [manner of] prayer and entreaty**......** AMP

The Goodspeed version says '***Use every kind of prayer and entreaty, and at every opportunity pray in the spirit.'***

Christians get themselves in a spot of bother by trying to make one kind of prayer for every situation they encounter. It's like playing every game/sport using football rules. Baseball, netball, basketball and football may all be ball games but they have different rules! Not only do you get confused when you try the one size fits all approach: you also don't get results. Too many folks want to suffix their prayer with a 'not mine but thy will be done.' How pious! That kind of prayer only works in a prayer of consecration, rededication where one is pouring his heart out, yielding to go anywhere and anyhow as the Lord leads. It's in stark contrast to the prayer of faith, where the will of God is known and the praying saint acts on the word! Prayer is not like the primal scream. It is talking with God to affect change in our spiritual lives and the world.

Interceding for the lost has its own rules and peculiarities.

The Travail of the Soul**.**

It is not a coincidence that some of the terms associated with intercession are agony, travail, grief, and groans. These terms are by and large used in the birth process.

Isaiah 66:8 says

Who hath heard such a thing? Who hath seen such things? Shall the earth be made to bring forth in one day? Or shall a nation be born at once? For as soon as Zion travailed, she brought forth her children.

Contrary to what others have said, the scripture does not refer to the rebirth of Israel only but to the church (which is symbolised by Zion) and her ability to bring forth children after a season of travailing. Paul says in Galatians 4: 19

My little children, of whom I travail again in birth, until Christ be formed in you.

Note the word '***again***' as it is used here. He had travailed to see to it that their souls were birthed into the kingdom of God (even though he needed to travail again for them). After his prayer they were born again. They did not just turn over a new leaf, but were born again: bringing sinners into the kingdom is not bereft of the labours and joys of child birth. Like our Lord Jesus, Paul had seen the fruit of the travail of his soul.

Isaiah 53 vs.11 says

He shall see the travail of his soul, and shall be satisfied.

One of the noisiest and liveliest places on planet earth is the maternity ward. There is a whole lot of groaning, pain, birth pangs, paroxysm and tears going on in there. Then there is the laughter, the relief and the glow which is majestic like the sudden burst of dawn, the glow in the east announcing the birth of a new day. A resounding note of victory echoed in heaven.

As soon as Zion travailed------,

If we don't travail, we don't plunder hell to populate heaven. We don't give birth to new moves of the Lord. We don't see revival. The birth imagery is well illustrated by the story of Elijah in Kings Chapter 18.

vs. 41

And Elijah said unto Ahab, Get thee up, eat and drink; for there is a sound of abundance of rain.

vs. 42 -------And Elijah went up to the top of Carmel; and he cast himself down upon the earth, and put his face between his knees,

vs. 43 and said to his servant, Go up now look toward the sea. And he went up and looked, and said,

There is nothing.

And he said, Go again seven times.

Vs.44 And it came to pass at the seventh time, that he said Behold, there ariseth a little cloud out of the sea, like a man's hand. And he said Go up and say to Ahab, Prepare thy chariot, and get thee down that the rain stop thee not.

vs. 45 and it came to pass in the meanwhile, that the heaven was black with clouds and wind, and there was great rain.

Elijah put his face between his knees------. Placing one's head between one's knees was a common practice of Oriental and Middle East women when they were about to give birth. Elijah's soul was incubating the heavy rains. He was in travail, hatching the rains. When the rains were in full term they poured forth!

If the clouds be full of rain, they empty themselves upon the earth.

Ecclesiastics 11:3

Are you incubating souls in the depths of your being? Are your bowels incubating a revival? Are you incubating church growth?

Charles Finney was one of America's greatest evangelists, ushering in more than half a million souls into the Kingdom of God in an age or epoch bereft of amplifiers and mass media communication. In the fledgling stages of his Christian walk, Charles Finney stumbled upon the precious truth of the travailing of the soul. He notes that in those early days the Lord taught him the importance of the spirit of prayer. Shortly after he was converted he had rented a room in one of the houses near his law office. The lady of the house was taken ill and the visibly agitated husband approached Charles Finney and stated that 'my wife cannot live through the night.' Charles Finney was immediately seized by a burden of prayer, which almost crushed him. So great was the burden that he left the office immediately and went to the meeting house to pray. He struggled and was seized by 'groanings' which were loud and deep. After agonising for a long time, with the breakthrough eluding him, he went back to the office but could not sit still. He paced the floor under the spirit of prayer and soon went back to the meeting house. Again he agonised in prayer. Words failed him and all he could do was weep and groan. He went to the office but could not rest. He went back to the prayer meeting a third time and this time the Lord gave him the power to prevail. He rolled the burden on the Lord and a knowing, an assurance came into his heart that the Lady will live and she wasn't going to die in her sins. He had an unwavering assurance. The Lady lived and soon gave her life to Christ. Charles Finney related this to a friend, remarking about the strangeness of the experience. The friend said to him,

'Why, that was the travail of your soul.'

<u>Why the Lord Ordained Travailing.</u>

Romans 8:22-23

22) For we know that the whole creation groaneth and travaileth in pain together until now.

23) And not only they, but ourselves also, which have the first fruits of the spirit, even we ourselves groan within ourselves, waiting for the adoption, to wit, the redemption of our body.

26) Likewise the spirit also helpeth our infirmities: for we know not what we should pray for as we ought: but the

Spirit itself maketh intercession for us with groanings which can not be uttered.

27) And he that searcheth the hearts knoweth what is the mind of the Spirit, because he maketh intercession for the saints according to the will of God.

Reidt's view on the above verses is insightful

'All creation is groaning and travailing in pain. The Ultimate consciousness of pain resides in God because of his perfect love. Through our fellowship with God we are brought into fellowship with the suffering creation.'

It is when we are united with the Lord's heart, in unison with him, that we acutely become conscious of the groaning of creation. We are crushed by the Father's burdened heart and by the sinner's sense of separation from the Lord. God is love. It is this perfect love that makes him acutely feel the pain and suffering of humankind/ creation. It is this love that has made many a saints break down before the Lord panting and agonising over lost souls.

The strength of the desires also stems from a sense of the clear and present danger the sinner faces. We are moved by the Holy Spirit inspired insight into the sinner's state and predicament.

The Lord will roll on the soul of the saint the burden to pray, the agony crushes his heart to powder, as he supernaturally experiences the chasm between the Lord and the sinner. The same chasm that made our Lord cry out on the cross,
'My Lord why have you forsaken me?!'

Our Lord of mercy, the Beneficent One allows such a predicament but does give the relief, the blessed assurance that victory has been granted and the sinner's heart will turn to his maker. The burden must however be rolled back to the Lord. Relief comes when the Holy Spirit is not quenched and we exercise childlike faith in the Lord.

When we are in the kingdom of God, and we are in fellowship with him, we also share the same pain and likewise groan with him. The Holy Ghost conveys God's sense of the suffering, the pain and helps us make intercession with groanings- groanings which cannot be uttered.

Soon after the first travail episode, another case presented itself to Charles Finney. There was a young Lady who was charming and well versed in the bible and religion. She remained unconverted however. Charles Finney and one of the Elders decided to agree that she will come to the Lord and they will bring her name to the Lord continuously in prayer. The Elder seemed to lose the 'spirit of prayer' with the passage of time. Unperturbed, Charles Finney continued to press the Lord on the issue. He then came across information that the Lady had become a Universalist. He was taken aback at first but the spirit of prayer like the one he had experienced with that sick Lady struck him like a crushing burden. He went to home to pray. He could not utter words but only came up with groans and tears. It seemed there was a cloud between him and the Lord to prevail upon her. He later said,

'The spirit struggled within me with groaning's that could not be uttered.'

He continued in travail at the crack of dawn and heard the Lord clearly saying 'yes, yes' as if in an audible voice. Suddenly the burden lifted and he was filled with joy and peace, feeling with certainty that her salvation was secure.'[Please note well, the note of victory again].

He misjudged the timing of her salvation however: The Lady gave her life to the Lord months down the line.

The Lord told me that without patience one will not win the good fight of faith.

Hebrew 6 v. 12 says

That ye be not slothful, but followers of them who through faith and patience inherit the promises.

Travailing can be viewed as a 'Lost Art' which is being restored to the church as the Lord is currently moving, changing the old into new. In essence, holy travail occurs when one or a group are gripped by the very burden gripping the Lord's heart. This results in a Holy Ghost inspired intense intercession as the Holy Spirit labours with our spirits to give both conception and vent to a new life. This accounts for the birth imagery that pervades travailing.

Once again the terms associated with giving birth are agony, anguish, pain, sweat, screams, push come to mind. Webster's dictionary gives an interesting definition of travail: very hard work, pains of childbirth. In churches where there is no travailing there is hardly any growth.

Intercession for the lost entails giving birth to new saints into the kingdom of God. Charles Finney's labours not only saw half a million souls come to the Lord but the majority of the new converts also stayed. Prayer enabled him to have abiding fruits. One of the secrets of Charles Finney's success was his intercession partner Father Daniel Nash. When Father Nash was led by the Lord to join Charles Finney in the regions of Evans Mills, New York, Finney noticed that Father Nash was full of the 'power of prayer.' The seemingly threadbare two man team had their evangelistic team premised on the fact that prayer was essential for evangelism. Often times Father Nash would go to an area three weeks prior to the meeting and 'prepare' the area for the meetings. He would enlist a few willing prayer partners and they would intercede for the souls to be birthed into the Kingdom during the revival meetings. That was the preparation for the area! They were binding the strong man of the area before entering it: Mark 3:27.

Charles Grandison Finney made a bold assertion: prevailing prayer seeks to influence man and also to move God. Not that this will change the Lord's position on anything or change his character and disposition: when we line up all the dynamics and factors together, the Lord is left with no choice but to act. Then there will be a performance from the most High God. For instance, the Lord is willing to forgive the sinner. It is however when the sinner get himself to a place of repentance that the Lord pleased by the sinner's meeting of the conditions of repentance will forgive the sinner and restore him into the kingdom. This obliquely echoes George Muller's observation that the Lord wants the believer to ask. The Lord does not only want us to seek answers, but to primarily seek his face. There is a Godward side and a 'man-ward' side to prayer. While deep in prayer, the Spirit changes our way of thinking, purges us of ignoble motives and makes us line up with heaven and reverberate with the heavenly impulse. When our 'Heavenly affections flow out- the soul rests sweetly and gloriously in God, and rejoices with joy unspeakable.' Finney observed.

Finney once chided a New York church saying that they are not capable of grasping the concept of travail because they are worldly, 'full of starch, pride and fashion and lack spirituality.' He warned them that they will never see a revival until they reach a place of brokenness before the Lord.

The state of the vessel is just as important as the efficacy of the vessel. Abraham was told

'I will make you great'

The Lord is in the business of 'making. '

Travailing brings brokenness and lines up the Christian with God's will. The blessing does not do him injury! He is not suddenly puffed up with pride. Travailing brings brokenness which deepens our spirituality bringing us closer to the Lord. Charles Finney, George Muller and a great number of God's Generals have noted how the person is more important to the Lord than the person's service. Travailing allows the Holy Spirit to mold us into what God wants us to be. That we give ourselves wholly to him and fall deeper in love with him.

Travailing and Perseverance.

One enduring quality of travailing is perseverance. To persevere one needs to fix one's mind on the promise until the blessing comes through. Focus is an essential component of travailing. Finney cautions against abandoning a prayer point before the reassurance of an answer in your spirit. Prevailing prayer is indeed a protracted process. One's mind gets exercised on the issue. One might go about his business or work but still continues to breathe out his desires to the Lord, praying under his breath. This is analogous to a loving mother with a sickly child. She might go into the next room, sweep or even 'doze off ' but her prayers and thoughts are with her child! Such a state of mind, one of perseverance and focus is indispensable in prevailing prayer.

The story of Jacob in Genesis 32:22-31 comes to mind. He cried out,
'I won't let you go until you bless me!'
Esau, whose birth right Jacob had stolen was coming for him with a fully-fledged army. The pungent smell of death hit Jacob's nostrils with the severity of a gunpowder's smell. He turned to the Lord all night. He needed divine intervention. All night, with a singularity of mind he wrestled with the Angel of the Lord. From thus came the spontaneous proclamation
I won't let you go till you bless me. In other words, I won't let you go till you give me my breakthrough!
Till you give me the assurance that you will see me through this turbulent time.

All night he had wrestled with the Angel of the Lord. At day break, emotionally spent and physically a wreck he got his breakthrough. The Angel blessed him, changed his destiny, and changed his walk, gaiety, his reach, his significance and his name.

Our Lord's sweat was like drops of blood as he prayed in the garden of Gethsemane.
It is said the Apostle James' knees were callous like a camel's knees by the time he met his demise. Praying Hyde is said to have prayed until his heart shifted in his chest. Charles Finney hailed the callous knees of what he called 'primitive ministers.'

Charles Finney tells the story of an aged blacksmith who lived in a town that had gone cold towards the Lord. The burden fell on him to pray for the town. He became so overpowered by the burden, he closed the shop and travailed until he got the breakthrough. He asked the local Minister to call an impromptu conference. The minister reluctantly agreed but hired a small hall since he did not have high hopes for the attendance.

The attendance was better than expected. They sat in silence for a while. Suddenly someone cried out for prayer. He had been under conviction for some time. And so were others. They soon cried out too. It was noted that the conviction began when the old blacksmith with a painfully severe speech impediment began to pray. Soon everyone in the town was crying out for salvation.

Charles Finney described a certain town near New York as a moral waste. Apostasy was evident. A midweek joint meeting of two churches had such a small attendance it was held in a private residence. Deacon M, an old man of a few words rose to pray. He started in a somewhat tepid fashion. As he prayed he took to standing on his toes and then falling on his heels. The jar went through the room. He was becoming more engaged, excitable and fervent. He was lifting a chair in front of him up and slamming it on the floor. Soon the whole room was crying out to the Lord. The cry set the town on fire for the Lord. The cry was soon echoed by surrounding towns.

Charles Finney gives an account of how he took a colleague with him to a grove to pray for the night service. After intense prayer they felt that they had 'prevailed with God' and that the power of the Lord will be revealed that night. And the power fell in that night's service. In the packed house Finney described the power of God as coming upon him like the opening of a battery. The word came down like fire and hammer upon a rock and there was great conviction in the church.
They saw the travail of their souls.
Soon after that Finney was to have his second encounter with Father Nash and they started to work together. He had seen him at the Presbytery where he was licensed. Soon after the chance meeting Father Nash was taken ill from the presbytery: he had inflamed eyes and had to be shut up in a dark room for weeks. Cut off from the capacity to read and write, he gave himself to prayer. When he regained his sight he devoted himself to labouring for souls.
He was full of power. The power of the Holy Ghost. He

had a 'prayer list' with names of people he was praying for to come to the Lord. Charles Finney was stuck by the man's faith and fruitfulness. In labours abundant, Father Nash would pray every day for the subjects of his prayer and sometimes many times a day. Finney described Father Nash's faith as 'almost miraculous.'

In that village lived a tavern owner a Mr D-who went about opposing the gospel and cursing Christians. Father Nash got to hear of this man, who was described as a tough case. Mr D-became Father Nash's subject of prayer. Father Nash soon moved to another area to continue in his labours. The notorious Mr D- turned up at the crowded church hall and caused no small stir. Finney kept an eye on him. It became evident that Mr D- had not come to cause trouble but was in a great anguish of mind peculiar to seekers. He was writhing in his seat and soon came forward tremblingly to confess. His comprehensive confession covered his attitude to the Lord, Christians and the revival. That broke fallow ground, bringing many to the Lord. The bar-room used for revelry became a venue for nightly prayers.

***God's timing*.**

It is important to note here that Mr D- came to the Lord while Father Nash was away. It did not bother Father Nash that he had to leave town and labour elsewhere before Mr D- gave his life to Christ. The times are in the Lord's hand. His ways are not our ways. I remember a time, when I was holding a revival in a certain place. The Lord impressed upon my heart that the church was going to grow and I needed to 'birth' this growth. From a

human standpoint of view this was next to impossible. The demographics were seriously unfavourable! The young and able bodied were emigrating en masse to more prosperous towns and the place was shrinking! Still, the Lord spoke of growth!
We walk not by sight but by faith.
I did leave the place, but my prayers did not lose their traction. With the passage of time, there was a sudden shift in demography and influential people in that society began to settle in that settlement. They gave their lives to the Lord and the place was spiritually galvanised. The word of God grew mightily and social groups which had traditionally been cold to the 'born again' message became receptive. They built a church and flourished. God's timing is perfect. God's time is the right time, George Muller was wont to say.
Hebrews 6:15 says
And so it was that he (Abraham), having waited long and endured patiently, realized and obtained (in the birth of Isaac as a pledge of what was to come) what God had promised him.
Amplified version.
Father Nash Profile

<u>The Spirit of Prayer.</u>
Evidently Charles Finney could not overemphasise the 'Agency ' of the Holy Spirit in the revival work in its entirety. It is the Holy Spirit who moves us to pray. It is the Holy Spirit who convicts. Charles Finney noted that there was a mighty Spirit of Prayer in his revivals. Many saints prayed and prevailed. Without the spirit of prayer,

our efforts are in vain. It is the Lord who through the power of the Holy Ghost does the work. Whenever the work came under threat the saints took the matter to the Lord seeking his intervention in turning events around in their favour. The results were tremendous. The Lord will never let us down.
As for himself, Finney said if he lost the 'spirit of grace and supplication for a day or even an hour' he would lose his ability to preach effectively and was fruitless in terms of winning souls through personal conversation.
Bareness stems from prayerlessness.

Importunity
God is no respector of persons. He however respects faith. Faith that persists in the face of adversity. He is the rewarder of those who diligently seek him.
Luke 11:5-8
And he said unto them, which of you shall have a friend and shall go unto him at midnight and shall say unto him Friend lend me three loaves; for a friend of mine in his journey is come to me, and I have nothing to set before him. And he from within he shall answer and say Trouble me not; the door is now shut, and my children are with me in bed; I cannot rise and give thee. I say unto you though he will not rise because he is a friend, yet because of his importunity he will rise and give him as many as he needeth.
Isaiah 62:6-7

I have set watchmen upon thy walls, O Jerusalem, which shall never hold their peace day nor night: ye

that make mention of the name of the Lord, hold not your silence.

Let us hold on to the Lord's words below
---because of his importunity he will rise and give him what he needeth……….

Properties of impunity.

1) Urgent need

The seeker_was in a predicament. A weary friend turning up at midnight. The Christian body is in a slumber because they don't sense the urgency to pray. When we are prayerful, the Holy Ghost will broadcast the Lord's consciousness of a creation groaning and suffering because of its separation from the Lord. As the whole creation moans, groans and travails so does our loving father. If we evil fathers do not smile when our children suffer how much more shall the living God be afflicted when his own children are afflicted. Prayerlessness stems from lack of a burden for the lost souls.

2) The seed of love

He had opened his door to his travelling friend and at midnight and gone the extra mile of visiting his neighbour to get some amenities. He had sown the seeds of love, self-sacrifice and comfort. Would he be denied his request? When we bury our self-seeking pursuits and selflessly travail for others shall the Lord not give us the harvest of an answered prayer?

3) Impotence

John Hyde (Praying Hyde as he was affectionately known) was fond of 2 Kings 4. In that portion of the scripture Elisha the prophet came against a widow. The

widow was not only facing starvation but she was about to lose her children to a creditor: she was in serious financial dire straits. She had only a pot of oil left, she told the Prophet. The Prophet told her to 'Go around and borrow vessels from all your neighbours, empty vessels- not a few.'
She did as she was told and witnessed a miracle as the remnant of the oil filled all the vessels.
Verse 6 says '***When the vessels were full, she said to her son, bring me another vessel. And he said There is not one left. And the oil stopped multiplying.' AMP***

The oil stopped multiplying. The lack of empty vessels stopped the miracle. We let miracles pass us by because we are too full of ourselves, our ambitions, plans, pursuits and priorities. We need to have this friend's sense of impotence: 'I have nothing to set before him.' College education alone will not do it. Experience alone will not do it. It is all by God's grace. Paul says in Galatians 8:2
(For he that wrought effectually in Peter to the apostleship of the circumcision, the same was mighty in me towards the Gentiles :)
Billy Graham said 'Prayer is crucial to evangelism: Only God can change the heart….No matter how logical or fervent our appeals, our words will accomplish nothing unless God's Spirit prepares the way.'
Zechariah 4:6 says
Not by might nor by power but by my spirit; says the Lord of Hosts.'

It is by his grace that we stand. Eloquence has no substance in soul winning. It is the prayerful preacher who will see many come to the Lord.

Persistence

Persistence is highly prized by the Lord, Andrew Murray tells us. Dr Lillian Yeoman said that nothing pleases God more than the sight of his children stepping out into a yawning gap with nothing to support them but the promises in his word.

HAVE FAITH IN GOD.

Charles Finney famously said,

'I was so exercised in prayer and had an experience that was somewhat new to me. I found myself so much exercised and so bourne down with the weight of immortal souls that I was constrained to pray without ceasing. Some of my experiences, indeed, alarmed me. A spirit of importunity sometimes came upon me so that I would say to God that he made a promise that he would answer prayer, and I would, not be denied.' (Finney 1977:105)

He felt so certain that his prayer will be answered, that the Lord was faithful to his promises and that it was impossible for God to lie and to let him down.

The promises of God are yes and amen.

The words of the Lord are pure words, like a silver tried in the furnace of the earth and purified seven times.

Romans 3:4 says

God Forbid: yeah, Let God be true, but every man a Liar...

In the twilight of his career, Charles Finney had the

opportunity to visit Europe. One night on his way back home, his mind was much exercised on the continuity of revivals. He feared that the revivals might die. His own health was failing and he did not know of anyone who could carry on the work. He was in utter agony. He paced up and down the deck.

He could not discuss his issue with anyone on board. His soul was crushed. He asked the Lord to 'provide himself with such instrumentalities ' as to continue the work. After a day of incredible wrestling, he prevailed. The Lord gave him assurance and rest. He knew it would be done. As to how it was to be done he had no idea. The Lord did answer him. A book entitled *Finney's Lectures on Revivals* was soon published and sparked revivals the world over. Charles Finney ascribed the ignition of the revival fires to the season of travailing on the homebound ship.

Yonggi Cho and the Law of Incubation.

Once again it is important to point out that the prayer warrior needs to stay on the prayer point until he sees the victory, until he has a knowing in his heart that his prayer has been answered.

The instant coffee mentality will not do in travailing. The Christian must be prepared to pray through to victory and after that stand firm in faith until what he or she is praying for becomes visible.

Hebrews 11:1 (KJV) says

Now faith is the substance of things hoped for, the evidence of things not seen.

When we stand believing, we stand in the best place to SEE the things hoped for come into visibility.

David Yonggi Cho espouses the Law of Incubation in his book *The Fourth Dimension* Volume one.

Yonggi Cho remembers the fledgling stage of his ministry when he struggled financially. He was still single. He had no bed, no desk, and no chair and walked for miles to win souls for the Lord. As he read the bible it was impressed upon his heart that the Lord does not want us to live like paupers bereft of material things and struggling financially. We are the children of the most High God, the King of Kings and Lord of Lords. Yonggi Cho asked the Lord for a humble chair, a desk, a humble bed and a bicycle to use for soul winning. He began to praise the Lord for the answer.

After six months though he didn't have the things he had asked for. Hungry and impoverished he enquired of the Lord. The Lord told him to be specific when making his request: Yonggi had asked for all these items but had not specified the type of items he really wanted. The Lord admonished him for being vague. His children had that same problem: vagueness. The Lord led him to Hebrews 11:1 ' –things hoped for.' Clear cut objects. A definite object, as Charles Finney put it. Yonggi Cho became specific in his request. In Mark 10 the Lord Jesus Christ asked Bartimaeus this question

'------What do you want me to do for you?'

The Lord had heard the man cry out for mercy and could tell that the man was blind. The visibly blind man told the Master

'That I might see.'

Now that's specificity.

He also got a startling revelation when he came across Romans 4 vs.17 and it dawned on him that God raises the dead and calls the things that be not as though they were.

He could start calling the things that be not as though they were!

He could adopt God's language. Talk about the things that were not as though they were. The Lord's promises yes and amen.

He announced to his church that he had by 'God's blessing a USA made bicycle; a desk made from Philippine mahogany, and a beautiful chair with iron frames and rollers on tips.' A few young men pressed him on the issue, wanting to see the goods. They even followed him to his office. Yonggi Cho bravely and painstakingly explained that the items were in his spiritual womb and will be visible to the world in due course, analogous to a child in her mother's womb for nine months. The young men burst out laughing. The idea of a pregnant man was a bit far-fetched to them. Incubation is a fitting birth imagery!The things Yonggi Cho was praying for came to him as an answered prayer. To God be the praise!

The promises of the Lord are yes and amen!

David Yonggi Cho sums up the law of incubation:

a) Have a definite, clear cut goal and objective

b) Have a burning desire

c) Pray until you get the assurance that you have got what you are praying for.

d) Start to call the things that be not as though they are : Romans 4 vs. 17

In due course all those things he was incubating in his spirit, became visible and tangible. We have a prayer answering God who will meet us at the point of need if we move along the lines of living faith.

Yes incubation is a befitting birth imagery.

Genesis 1:
1. In the beginning God created the heaven and the earth
2. And the earth was without form and void; and darkness was upon the face of the deep. And the Spirit of the Lord moved upon the face of the waters
The Amplified version says in the beginning ***God (prepared, formed, fashioned the heavens and the***

earth….The Spirit of God was moving (hovering, brooding) over the face of the waters.' (Genesis 1:1, 2). The word move in Hebrew is 'Rachaph' which means to brood or to flutter. To brood is to 'sit over something so as to hatch.' Pastor Chris rightly notes. The Spirit was not moving randomly and aimlessly. It was brooding over the earth to hatch! After brooding, after covering and after sitting on the earth to hatch things the Lord said 'let there be light!'

And there was light. And the Lord saw that it was good. That is how the power of the creative force he gave us works. We hatch the things we desire by sitting over them in spirit filled prayer. We let our regenerated spirit together with the Holy Ghost sit over the issue, the desire, the prayer request as we wait for the fullness of time. We keep ourselves fixed and focused on the issue. In due season our spirit will bring forth into the material world that which we are agonising over. Are you brooding over the promotion you are seeking? Are you brooding over that lost soul? Let your spirit be burdened by the prayer request. Pray in tongues over the issue. Speak you victory over the issue. Victory will burst forth onto the scene.

The Lord said 'Let the earth bring forth grass, the herb yielding seed…and it was so.'

His words brought this herbs into being. He used his words only. Before he spoke though, he was meditating, incubating deeply. He was sitting over the issue so as to hatch. Speak scriptures over your issue. See the hand of the Lord over your circumstances until you sense a shift in the spiritual world. In his book *Recreating Your*

World, Pastor Chris urges the Saint to spend time in prayer until he/she get visions in your spirit. You must brood over the dreams until you are so fired up with the word of God that speak forth the word that will bring it to pass. When you catch an idea through the power of the Holy Ghost, let it fill your thoughts. Let it change and charge your confessions. The idea must be strong and overwhelming in you. You pray over it, confess victory until you start to visualise yourself in that desired position. You start to call the things that be not as if they are there. There is need to spend more time in prayer to bring the ideas into materialisation. The spirit of the Lord was creating in the midst of the darkness and chaos. The earth was a chaotic mass. Still the Spirit of the Lord was creating. The power to create is in you. Brood over your dreams in the midst of chaos, darkness, illness, scarce, economic turmoil and all the negative forces one can encounter. The power to create will breakthrough all the hindrances.

CHAPTER THREE: WEAPONISING YOUR TONGUE BY ARMING IT WITH THE WORD OF GOD.

Once you have the assurance in your heart that there is a breakthrough in what you have prayed for, do undo the victory by doubts and negative confessions. This will abort the 'child' in the spiritual world waiting for its due season to enter the material world or be discernible according to human notions of reality.

Hold Fast To Your Confession of Victory.

A story is told about how Smith Wigglesworth read from the portion of scripture which says [Mark 11vs 23] 'for he shall have whatsoever he sayeth.' He then challenged the members,

'Are you sayething?'

He asked the challenging questions several times. After the service he retired to the home of his host, Reverend George Stormont. After the note of victory in prayer, do not undo your victory by making negative confessions. After shouting their victory the Saints of God may nullify their victory through doubt and acts which do not correspond to their proclamation of victory.

For verily I say unto you , that whosoever shall say unto this mountain, Be thou removed and be thou cast into the sea and shall not doubt in his heart but shall believe that those things which he saith shall come to pass; he shall have

whatsoever he saith.
Mark 11vs 23

The Host told Smith Wigglesworth,

'There is no such a word as sayething.'

Smith Wigglesworth replied,

'Young man, do you know what you need to do? You need to go down on your knees and pray until you start sayething!'

Confession, positive confession is a fundamental principle in the walk of faith, as KEH would emphasize. Like E.W Kenyon, he sought to distinguish between confession as commonly used in confession of sin and confession as used in the context of professing or saying and that's right, sayething!

According to E.W Kenyon Christianity is called the 'Great Confession'. Confession is affirming something that we believe. It is testifying about something that we believe. It is testifying about something that we know. It is witnessing for a truth that we have embraced. Confession holds a very large place in Christianity.

Hebrews 10:23 says Let us hold fast the profession of our faith without wavering; (for he is faithful that promised ;)

Not too many preachers of living faith can say they have not, in some way been touched by E.W Kenyon's dynamic ministry. KEH is not an exception especially when it comes to positive confession. Hebrews 4:14 also says 'let us hold fast to our confession.'

After reading Hebrews 4:14 Kenyon asked the question

'What confession am I supposed to hold on to?.' [Gosset and Kenyon: 1981]

He found that he was to hold fast to the redemptive work of Calvary; hold fast to the confession that he was a new creature who had received the life and nature of God. We are to hold fast to the confession that God is the strength of our lives. I am to hold fast to the confession that

'Surely he hath borne my sickness and carried my disease, and that by his stripes I am healed.'

That God is the strength of my life.

Kenyon also says what I confess, I possess.

KEH premises his confession discourse on the book of Proverbs 6:2

'***Thou art snared with the words of thy mouth. Thou art taken captive with the words of your mouth***.'

If you confess lack, then lack will come. Your tongue will stop the inflow of money. If you confess doubt, doubt will rise like a giant and hold you in bondage. Words are not empty carriers. They contain your faith or your doubts. Curses or blessings. Want or plenty.

For verily I say unto you , that whosoever shall say unto this mountain, Be thou removed and be thou cast into the sea and shall not doubt in his heart but shall believe that those things which he saith shall come to pass he shall have whatsoever he saith.

Whatsoever he saith. It might be life or Death. Success or failure. Victory or defeat.

Words contain your faith or your doubts.

For verily I say unto you , that whosoever shall say unto this mountain, Be thou removed and be thou cast into the sea and shall not doubt in his heart but shall believe that those things which he saith shall come to pass he shall have whatsoever he saith.

Words contain your supply or your want. Life or Death. Success or failure. Victory or defeat.

In his pastoral days on Tuesdays and Thursdays Brother Hagin would prayerfully read the book of Mark. For some reason Mark was his favorite Gospel. It might have been something to do with him being healed from an incurable blood disease and two serious organic heart diseases that left him practically paralyzed after standing on Mark 11 vs.23, 24 when he was a teenager. He prayed, pacing up and down the aisles of the church, meditating on the Word of God. That day in that small Texas town, he meditated on the great commission in Mark 16. He was by now on his knees. He got up, and sat down. His mind was much exercised along the lines that the signs are supposed to follow when we go out to preach. He sat still before the Lord.

Psalms 46:10 says 'Be still and know that I am God.'

When he got to the place where his mind was quiet, he heard a voice rise from deep down his spirit.

The words were so clear, so real, so plain it was like someone was talking to him. The voice pointed out that in the book of mark 11 vs 23 the word 'say' had been used three times in some form or another, yet the word pray had been used just once. KEH had read Mark 11 vs 23, his keynote scripture ,thousands of times but he had not noticed that fact. The bible was ours to take-with our heart. Trying to understand it with your head was futile, KEH would say. He told the Lord that he had not noticed that 'say' was used three times while believe was only used once.

For verily I say unto you , that whosoever shall say unto this mountain, Be thou removed and be thou cast into the sea and shall not doubt but shall believe that those things which he saith shall come to pass he shall have whatsoever he sayeth.

Mark 11:22,23

A eureka moment it was, humanly speaking. The Lord then said to KEH, my people are not missing it primarily in their believing. They are missing it in saying. They have been exposed to other teachings but not on saying. Faith must however be released by words which come through the mouth.

You can have whatever you say.

It suddenly dawned on KEH that of all the ministers he had

heard preaching, no one had preached about the 'saying' aspect. The Lord told him that he would have to preach three times more on saying than on believing. KEH checked himself and began to preach more on saying.

Mark 11 says and '*shall not doubt in his heart but shall believe that those things which he saith...*'

You have to believe in what you are saying. Those words become powerful and fruitful. If you believe what you say whether it's negative or possible it will come to pass. There is no point in believing God for something then talk negatively, talking unbelief. You will just be cancelling your faith position! You will be preempting your prayer and rendering your prayer sterile. Few people realize just how words dominate our lives, KEH would frequently say. A Christian must never talk failure. He must never talk defeat.

On the 22nd of February 1965 at Pasadena Texas in Manning Street, Reverend Hagin preached at Brother Goodwin's church on 'Holding Fast To Your Confession.'

This is the gist of what he said.

The young travelling Evangelist started by encouraging the congregants to make time to hear the word. There is a reward that comes with making time to hear the word of God. He cited the example of a couple who had a problem and had attended one of his meetings. They were Baptists who had never heard of or had any Pentecostal experience before. It was all new. The husband took a 3 week vacation. His Boss was alright with it but wondered why he was taking time off so early in the year. The Baptist man replied that it was to go to church. They had seen KEH's advert and were keen to attend the service. His wife was afflicted by an incurable condition. His decision paid dividends because his wife was healed of the incurable disease. 'We get things out of balance,' he said. We win victories not by works but by faith. People believe the wrong things. Let us hold fast to our confession.' [1965 Hold Fast to Your Confession Tape].

KEH said that he noticed that in his life and other people's lives there was a continual sense of failure. He knew from experience that God heals. There was a leakage somewhere. God heals but why were folks failing in their bid to be healed? The Lord showed him where the leakage was and the cure for it. The Lord after all knows everything. His wisdom was infinite. In the sermon he pointed out that the spirit knows everything. The spirit of man is the candle of the Lord. God uses your own spirit to enlighten you. You switch on the light to see. The Lord shows you things through your own spirit. The leak was not holding fast to one's confession. What confession am I to hold on to? The integrity of the scriptures. Hold fast to the fact that you are a new creature. Hold fast to the fact that God is the strength of your life. Hold fast to the fact that he has borne our diseases, by his stripes we were healed. Hold fast to the confession. Hold fast to your confession even if physical evidence is contrary. We must not have sense rules minds which don't settle on the word. We must say it is done even if the enemy is saying something to the contrary.

It is difficult to hold fast to one's confession when the symptoms of illness persist. God has not given you a promise to heal you in the future. Himself took our infirmities. It is done. It's all in the past tense. A promise is in the future. Healing is a gift. It has been done for you. It is in the past.

'Friends I say it with tears. I have seen preachers and wives die saying I will be healed,' [Hold Fast to Your Confession Tape 1965.] Faith is not future tense it is present tense. By his stripped I am healed. By his stripes you were healed. If you were healed then you are healed. If you were paid for January's work then you were paid. It has been done. People have two confessions. They confess the truth about their symptoms and also confess the truth of the Word of God. Dr Yeomans, wrote a chapter in 1930 called 30 years of divine health. Someone said to her

'Please pray for my cold.'

She roared out,

'Your cold? Your cold?'

Dr Yeoman had the voice of a man. She said there was no use for praying for it. After finishing praying for it he will just have it as long he claimed that the cold was his.

You are the custodian of your body. The body your house. You can tell Satan not to live there.

'I am not taking a cold, it is a healthy sneeze.' KEH was wont to say.

Hold fast to your confession. The confession of the word's position on your situation. Don't say yes the Lord has healed me, then turn around and make a confession about how the symptoms continue to persist.

A negative confession is tantamount to taking sides against the Word of God.

The Lord is my shepherd, I shall not lack.

Suddenly, in that service, Mrs. Goodwin spoke in tongues. Her Husband Rev. Goodwin interpreted.

'*This is what I have said in my word, all I have given unto you is yours to take------you don't need to wait until you receive or see the manifestation--- rejoice before you see the results. You miss them because you receive them not. I have given them into your hand.'*

The crowd broke into spontaneous prayer.

Mrs Goodwin spoke again in tongues.

Interpretation: *Now you might see as you see records of many who have to come to me when it looked impossible, but they received because they rejoiced before they saw them.*

He weighs your heart daily and rewards those who receive his word fully.'

Again the church was galvanised, breaking spontaneously into prayer.

KEH prophesied '*if thou will say he is my helper...surely thou will not fall. He holds you--- plead not your ignorance—*

he has given you light—so you will not come behind in any way---thou shall climb and climb , the heavenly breezes shall be a thing to enjoy. Thy spirit and soul, tongue and mouth shall be full of shout--------'

The church broke into spontaneous prayer one more time. KEH urged the church to confess that Jesus is mine. 'Confess that he is your shepherd you shall not lack.'

Mrs Goodwin spoke in tongues again.

Brother Goodwin interpreted.

'*Why seek ye for that which is not lost, **it is near thee even in thy mouth**---come with one purpose that which is written , set down by the holy spirit---these things which are eternal these things which are strong, and mighty to you and in your very spirit, to overcome all the enemy and trample him down on your feet as I have declared.*'

KEH spoke in tongues.

Papa Goodwin : *Now say it say ,--my need is supplied. Take it. Take it in faith. I declare his truth. I refuse to be moved. I will hold to his word and to his truth. If I look upon others who fail. I too will----groan in in my sprit saying o you don't understand my situation—the complexes you do not understand what I am going through. But I say unto you to arise, ---preach my word, preach it yourself, o preach it to the walls---God is and is a rewarder of those who diligently seek him and therefore I walk with God.*

The spirit moved in the church.

It was a powerful service.

***For verily I say unto you , that whosoever shall say unto this mountain, Be thou removed and be thou cast into the sea and shall not doubt but shall believe that those things which he saith shall come to pass ,he shall have whatsoever he saith*.**

Mark 11:23

The Word pray is not used at all in verse 23

. It is used in Mark 11:24

24. ***Therefore whatsoever you desire, when ye pray believe that you receive them and you shall have them.***

In verse 23 one can see faith working with saying only. After praying you still have to say it. After praying for his healing, KEH said 'I am healed.' You still have to speak your healing, confess the word of God. On the deathbed as a teenager, after praying for his healing, he began to ***say*** out that he had been healed. He began to make the declaration, 'I believe I am healed—I receive healing for my body from the crown of my head to the soles of my feet.'

He believed it and he ***said*** it. The Lord Jesus said you shall have whatsoever you say. After saying it, the symptoms disappeared within an hour. KEH was always quick to point out that symptoms don't always disappear that fast but in his situation, they did. Hebrews 4:14 says '----let us hold fast to our confession.' That's not talking about sin. Its confession/profession of the word of God. When you confess your sin, the Lord forgives you, so why do you have to hold on to it? It's about confessing that you have what the Lord says you have. When you believe that you have received money from the Lord you need to keep confessing that. Keep confessing that you have it. KEH said at times it has been days before the money came. At times it has been weeks. At times months or even years. But Thank God it always came. He was wont to say that God does not settle up every Saturday. Hold fast to your confession. In *Mountain Moving Faith*, KEH cites Romans 4:18,19,

17) (As it is written, I have made thee a father of many nations). Before him whom he believed, even God, who quickeneth the dead, and calleth those things which be not as though they were.

18***) Who against hope in hope believed, that he might become the father of many nations, according to that which***

was spoken, so shall they seed be. KJV

[19] He did not weaken in faith when he considered the[utter] impotence of his own body which was as good as dead as he was about a hundred years old or [or considered] the barrenness of Sarah's [deadened] womb.

20) No doubt or unbelief made him waver ---concerning the promise of God, but he grew strong and was empowered by faith as he gave praise and glory to the Lord.

21) Fully satisfied that God was able and mighty to keep his word and to do what he had promised.

Amplified Classic

Abraham believed the word he heard from the Lord. He did not believe what he was seeing. He was not walking by sight.

He confessed that he who had promised was well able to deliver. He believed that God had already done it and started to praise him and give glory to him. He was not walking by sight but by faith. Smith Wigglesworth is famous for saying

'I am not moved by what I see. I am only moved by what I believe.'

As a young Baptist boy KEH had hastily scribbled the Baptist motto on the flyleaf of his Grandmother's bible: 'The bible says it, I believe it and that settles it.'

When animosity strikes, and you are in a hard place just stand on the word of God, don't be moved by sight . Don't undo your prayer by confessing defeat. The Farmer does not reclaim his seeds from the ground just because the rains have delayed. Confess your victory. 'This will bring you out of a hard place.' he said in his book Mountain Moving Faith.

Always in the face of the impossible, the Holy Spirit has always helped me to see that he who smote the red sea and the children of Israel crossed the red sea as if on dry land is the same yesterday, today, tomorrow and forever! Isaiah 59:19 says

-----. When the enemy shall come in like a flood, the spirit of the Lord shall lift up a standard against him.

The Holy Spirit charges our faith to an extent that the enemy cannot stand. Jude says

'***But ye, beloved, building up yourselves on your most holy faith, praying in the Holy Ghost***,

Praying in the Holy Ghost builds up our faith. The Greek word for denotes 'charging like a battery.' When we pray in the Holy Spirit we charge ourselves and faith like a charging battery. Not praying in the Spirit leaves us flat, wobbly and ineffectual in the face of the enemy. We are left naked to the enemy.

CHAPTER 4: Praying Without Ceasing and Waiting Upon the Lord.

Spending Time in the Presence of the Lord

Kenneth E Hagin says stressed the importance of waiting upon the Lord to get revelation and divine guidance. Benny Hinn talks about practicing the presence of the Lord. Being in the presence of the Lord, fellowshipping with him and enjoying your oneness with him.

But they wait upon the Lord shall renew their strength: they shall mount up with wings as eagles; they shall and not be weary and shall walk not faint.

KEH states that he got most of his revelations by just waiting upon the Lord. We have a talking God. As we spend time waiting upon him, worshipping, reading the scriptures prayerfully and seeking his face, he will start to talk to your spirit. He will start to give you counsel. His spirit will start to break you, sensitise you to the urges and impulse from heaven. Divine guidance comes through.

They that wait upon the Lord shall renew their strength. Renewal entails removal of the old, the impure the outdated and replace with the new stronger and up to date. As we wait upon the Lord the weariness withers, the deranged compass is re-adjusted. We fall in line with God's strength.
They shall mount up with wings as eagles.
When an eagle is tired, it goes and rests on a rock. It spreads its wings and allows the wind to lift it up and carry it away. The direction is dictated by the wind.
The rock represents Jesus, the living word and the scriptures, his written word. When we rest on the word. When we have the firm foundation of the word undergirding our prayer. When we sit still before the Lord meditating on his promises the spirit will begin a work in us. He will start to stir us up. As we become yielded to him we start to soar like an eagle. We rise above carnality and doubts. We rise into a position where we cannot be denied and at that level; The Lord is more real than the material world. Up there, the eagle sees things differently. Waiting upon the Lord changes our perspective. The eagle can spot a serpent miles away when it's up there. Up there we can see the enemy and stop him in his tracks.

We are in a spiritual battle. Let's place ourselves at a vantage point where the enemy's weaknesses are laid bare to us.
They shall walk and faint.
This sounds like an anti-climax. They shall mount up, then they shall walk.
It's not an anti-climax Benny Hinn observed.

The walk is the end. The mounting and running are the means.
We aim to walk in the light of his guidance.

Come o house of Jacob let us walk in the light of the Lord.
We aim to have longevity in the Lord.
They shall walk and not be weary
We aim to be in line in agreement with him
How can two walk together unless they agree? Formatting a disk means to make it compatible with the computer. This entails removing some material and adding some material. When we are before the Lord we are formatted by the Holy Ghost to be what the Lord wants us to be.

When you are in God's presence, the God elements rubs into you. Smith Wigglesworth was a man of prayer. Once he was travelling by train to a convention. He accessed the bathroom for a short season of pray. On coming out of the bathroom, the clerk jumped out and screamed

'You convince me of sin!'

Soon the whole train was screaming for salvation. Waiting upon the Lord fills us with his presence and the world can Christ in us. Charles Finney visited a factory once. As he stood on the shop floor he noticed a young woman begin to agonise under conviction. He started to walk towards her and she broke under the conviction of the Lord. Soon the whole factory was crying out for mercy. The presence of the Lord shone in his face. Moses' face shone as he talked to the Lord (Exodus 34:29).

Gertrude Lake Reidt, a long time intercessor noted that a life of fruitful prayer entails isolation, self-denial, and perseverance.

Benny Hinn talks about creating an atmosphere that is surcharged with God's presence. You can put on a tape and meditate on the word of in a worshipping mode. There in that presence the Lord will reach out to you. Remember he dwells in the praises of his people.

Those close to KEH remember that he loved playing and watching baseball. Still, even if he was watching baseball, one could observe KEH's lips moving: he would be praying in tongues. It reminds one of Paul's claim,

'I thank God, I speak in tongues more than you all.'
He lived the scripture 'Pray without ceasing.'
Mighty miracles are either wrought or lost depending on our ability to sense God's burden and pray.
John Wesley once observed that it seemed as if God does not do anything unless the saints pray.
'It seems that God is limited by our prayer lives, he can do nothing for humanity unless someone asks him to do it.' KEH would often quote John Wesley.

If you have a burden to pray for something, stay with it, praying until it (the burden) lifts. This, he would say several times. A lot of folks wonder why it seems like God does not talk to them. They just go on their knees pray in tongues a bit and walk away. No. Believers must be willing to pray long enough, stay in prayer and the Lord will use them. It won't do to leave the place of prayer and go on your day to day business without having heard from God. There is need to spend time fellowshipping with the Lord. That way you make yourself more and more available for God to use you. KEH states that if you spend extra time praying, when the Lord is just looking for someone to pray about a particular issue or person, he will choose you.

At one time, like on several occasions, Reverend Kenneth E Hagin had an urge to pray. He sensed that someone was in danger. Whenever he had this feeling, he would pray until he sensed a breakthrough or a spirit of happiness and laughter. At that time they had Oral Roberts University students at his house. He suddenly sensed the urgent need to pray for someone whose life was in danger. One of the students, evidently in distress told them to pray for her father. Her mother had called to say that on that particular day there has been an explosion at the oil refinery where her father worked. All men were trapped in that raging inferno. Reverend Hagin rallied the troops and prayer was made until they hit that note of victory. All the men in the refinery survived, consistent with the word of prophecy that came during the prayer. The young lass, her mother and father all came to train at Rhema Bible College afterwards.

KEH remembered the time when he heard that Pat's Momma, (pet name for his mother) was not feeling well. He called her Pastor, Brother Wood, to find out how his mother was doing. Pastor Wood, advised KEH to come and see her because the situation was fast deteriorating. She faced certain death. As was his custom KEH began to pray in tongues, pleading with the Lord. He reminded the Lord that she was only 68, and had known nothing but poverty all her life. Now he was in a position to help her, he surely couldn't take her from him. Could he let her live to be eighty years old? The Lord pled his side back, telling him, he, KEH couldn't carry her on his faith forever. She had been stuck in the baby Christian phase for too long a time. She was better off coming home. KEH told the Lord about his love for her and how he was unable to let go of her just yet. Could she live up to eighty? The Lord acquiesced and his Mother went on to live for 80 years and 2 weeks. In the intervening period she had received the Holy Spirit and spoke in tongues. She also went on to have a glorious 'homecoming'.

Waiting Upon the Lord and Revelation.

1 Corinthians 2: 9 says

'But as it is written, Eye hath not seen, nor ear heard, neither have entered into the heart of man, the things which God hath prepared for them that love him.'

This scripture is not about things the Lord has prepared in the distant future which we can't know. The revelation of great things comes as we wait upon the Lord. KEH maintained that the Lord has prepared a great treasury of wisdom but the Body of Christ misses out by not walking in the spirit. 1 Corinthians 2:9 again,

'But as it is written, Eye hath not seen, nor ear heard, neither have entered into the heart of man, the things which God hath prepared for them that love him.'

Thus scripture is not about things the Lord has prepared for us in heaven, KEH contends. Verse 10 states that

'***But God has revealed them unto us by his Spirit, for the Spirit searcheth all things, yeah the deep things of God.***'

Here Paul is talking about the Lord revealing things through the spirit and not our natural senses. It was the Holy Spirit who gave Paul the revelation of the new redemption plan, and also the revelation of the mysteries of God hidden to the world for many ages. KEH knew this from experience because the Lord had given him revelation by praying for hours on end in the spirit. He remembered a time in the early days of his ministry when he could quote three quarters of the scripture from the top of his head. They used to call him the talking bible. He would rattle them out so fast in his preaching the congregation would urge him to slow down. They couldn't follow him.

When he started to pray in tongues on a daily basis, fellowshipping with the Lord the bible became alive to him and supernatural revelation came to him.

The portion of the scripture in 1 Corinthians 2:10-13 is particularly instructive,

10*) '*But God hath revealed them what he has prepared for us unto us by his Spirit: for the Spirit searcheth all things, yea, the deep things of God.

11) For what man knoweth things of a man, save the spirit of man which is in him? Even so the things of God knoweth no man, but the Spirit of God.

12) Now we have received, not the spirit of the world, but the Spirit of which is God, that we might know the things which are freely given to us of God.

13) Which things also we speak, not in the words which man's wisdom teacheth, but which the Holy Ghost teacheth, comparing spiritual things with the spiritual.

These scriptures, KEH said, were fulfilled in his life. The Lord would take him through the scriptures, examining two chapters or so and revelation would come to him. He would start to see things in a different light. He said,

'I'll say it again- the primary knowledge I have gained from the Bible, I didn't get it by reading someone's book. The deeper things of the Word of God I learned on my knees by praying in other tongues.' [See Kenneth E Hagin: Tongues Beyond The Upper Room.]

Oral Roberts also talks about how he read the entire four Gospels and the book of Acts on his knees praying. The word of God is inseparably interwoven with the Holy Ghost. To understand the word we need revelation from the Holy Ghost who moved man of old to write the scriptures. Reidt stated that dullness of perception is an infirmity. Through the power of the Holy Spirit, we can overcome that infirmity as we spend time praying in the spirit and meditating on the word of God. 1 John 2:20 says

But ye have the unction from the Holy One, and you know all things.

The unction unveils the truth. Paul says in the book of Ephesians 1: 16-20

16 {I}Cease not to give thanks for you, making mention of you in my prayers;

17 That the God of our Lord Jesus Christ , the Father of glory may give unto you the spirit of wisdom and revelation in the knowledge of him

18 The eyes of your understanding being enlightened; that ye might know what is the hope of his calling, and what are the riches of the glory of his inheritance in the saints

19 And what is the exceeding greatness of his power to us-ward who believe according to the working of his mighty power

20 Far above all principality, and power and might and dominion , and every name that is named, not only in this world, but also in that which is to come:

It is the spirit which gives us revelation of the hidden treasures of the scriptures. Smith Wigglesworth said

'*Seek God until you get a mighty revelation of his Son*

which puts you in a place where you are always steadfast in every circumstance.'

KEH remembers how he had done well for almost 12 years in the ministry. He was pastoring in east Texas then. The Church he was pastoring loved him. He was not struggling financially. The sanctuary was full every Sunday night. Still, he was dissatisfied. He devoted more time to prayer and fasting. He would fast for the whole day or he would simply skip a meal or two. He asked his family not to disturb him so that he could isolate himself to pray and fellowship with the Lord. He spent many hours on his knees praying for himself over and over again, employing Ephesians 1:15-23 and Ephesians 3: 14-21. He kept his bible open all the time, praying those prayers and inserting his name in them. He would wait before the Lord, at times in silence and at times he would burst into tongues. He sought God, wanting to identify that sense of dissatisfaction.

As he waited thus on the Lord, he would get in the realm of the spirit. It was as if he was digging deep into his spirit, removing things and laying them on the alter.

He laid the question on the alter 'why am I dissatisfied?'

The Lord told him the restlessness was because there was something else he was supposed to be doing and he was not doing it. He kept waiting on the Lord and soon there was a long line of things on the alter which he had taken out of himself. At last he seemed to have gotten down to the bottom of things. Still something came out. It was an old wrinkly thing which looked like a black shoe that had been in the rain. It had tentacles sticking out of it like an octopus. The Lord said it was some of his old denominational traditions. KEH was wont to say 'I was born and raised a Southern Baptist until they gave me the left foot of fellowship.' He thought he had gotten rid of his Southern Baptist traditions, but alas! He was yet to get rid of all of them. There was also to come out some Pentecostal traditions which were not biblical. They didn't look wrong but they didn't look quite right either. They too had to go. One day, as he prayed in tongues the Lord said to him, I am going to take you on to visions and revelations.

This was in the winter of 1947 and 1948. In six months' time the revelation of the word of the Lord began to come to him. He wondered out aloud to Oretha 'what have I been preaching about all these years?' By the end of 1948, he had learnt more about the bible than he had in all the pastoral years put together.

Waiting on the Lord also led him to the powerful revelation on prosperity. Remember at that time prosperity was a dirty word and an abomination. These were the early fifties. Small town piety dictated that the Saints become averse to the riches of the world. A season of waiting on the Lord yielded dividends for the diligent servant of God.

Oral Roberts' talks about how he struggled in the early days of his ministry. He remembered how at times his wife Evelyn had to offload some items from the trolley at the till because she was short of the money to pay for the bare necessities she would have gone to shop for. He engaged the church board on the issue, giving them a detailed income and expenditure statement. He even included his haircut.

Gives a whole new meaning to splitting hairs!

Still the raise did not do much to alleviate his suffering. Then one day when he was rushing out of the house, in the morning to go to College, he 'accidentally' came across 3 John 1:2

'Beloved I wish above all that thou mayest prosper and be in health even as thy soul prospereth.'

Both him, and Evelyn couldn't believe their eyes.

The Lord wanted them to prosper!

The revelation of prosperity came to them that day.

Kenneth W Hagin bears witness to the grinding poverty they had to endure in the fledgling stages of his father's ministry. In how God taught me about prosperity, Kenneth E Hagin asserts that he got the revelation on prosperity from the Lord himself: he did not get it from a book. Needless to say such an assertion would go on to raise the ire of heresy hunters like the Dale H. Simmons. Kenneth Hagin explicitly states that he got the Revelation from heaven itself.

Kenneth E Hagin was born and raised a Southern Baptist and saw at first hand their doctrine of 'poverty is divinity'; small time piety, more so when the first church he pastored was Baptist. Their pseudo philosophy was 'keep him poor Lord and we will keep him humble.'

Lending God a helping hand?

He then went over to the Pentecostals who bubbled with vim, vigour and vitality and still he found them two hundred fold better at keeping their pastor down at the end of the' -Get Along Street' right next to Grumble Alley. In church tjhere are Saints and there are 'Aints!' KEH would put it in his homespun, folksy good ole boy style. Their perspective was built on fallacious grounds.

In the early twenty first century, they wrongly premised their view on the fallacious grounds that money is the root of all evil. Actually the scriptures did not say money is the root of all evil: it said the ***love of money*** is the root of all evil. There was nothing wrong with money per se. Of course we must shun filthy lucre. Smith Wigglesworth, well known for being austere only pledged to be faithful to the call if the soles of his shoes were not worn out; his white shirt did not look suspiciously off white and he did not have to wear his trousers with his knees out! He would go back to plumbing if the provision condition was not met. A friend had remarked to him that 'All the people who say they live by faith seem to have their heels worn out, and their clothes are old and green.'

Wigglesworth is reported to have said that he believed that 'God would abundantly provide if I served him faithfully.'

It is possible for one to believe God for power to raise the dead yet have no faith in believing God for a single dollar: the early Hagin was no exception. He endured more than 12 years of poverty. He would say from the pulpit about that poverty stricken era: he went through life only through the medium of 'kicking, clawing, bawling and squalling.'

On a moment of reflection, he found that after February 1949 (when he made his excursion into the field) he was out by $1200.00. The home churches he had pastored had always taken care of him: furnished the pastorate; bankrolled his spiritual development at conventions; paid the utilities bills; furnished them with greens and flesh; showered the family with gifts. From a man's point of view, going into the field as an evangelist was a turn for the worst financially.

Kenneth Hagin reports that during the first year in the field, his clothes and car were worn out. The car ran on 4 bold tires and nothing to spare: how emotionally tiring! So overused the car was he could not sell it as a used car but as junk. His cash inflow was barely enough to pay interest on the bond he had taken out. The principal was untouched. Net of school clothes for the children he was down to zero.

Nothing is as dispiriting to the heart of a father as failing to provide for his loved ones. They lived in a 3 bedroom apartment that did not boast of a bedroom for young Ken. The poor boy had to contend with a kitchen based rollaway bed.

In his small book *What God Taught Me about Prosperity* he talks about how things came to a head when he was conducting a meeting in East Texas, and he poured his heart before the Lord concerning his financial state.

He went on a partial fast and availed himself for hours on end to the lord in prayer. He talked to the lord the way he talked to the next person: no need to intone your voice, put up airs after all the Lord knows your voice! On the third day he laid bare his financial transactions before the Lord and told the Lord that he was better off based in a local church. He had fastened on the scripture which said,

'If ye be willing and obedient, ye shall eat the good of the land,' (Isaah 1:19).

He brought it to the Lord's remembrance, not as if the Lord was an amnesic geriatric, but brought the promise to him whose promises and words were like ***'Silver tried in a furnace on the earth, purified seven times.'***

(Psalms 12:6)

He chronicled his fast deteriorating situation suffixing his plea with reference to the Lord's promise, ye shall eat the good of the Land'

He told the Lord, he was not eating. the good of the land surely!

Isaiah 1:19 says

If ye be willing and obedient, ye shall eat the good of the land.'

Then like he spoke to Elijah, the Lord spoke in a still small voice. The Lord told him plainly that he, Kenneth, did not qualify. The assertion shook Hagin to his roots. He said 'lord you hit me a low blow there'.

The Lord gently explained to Brother Hagin

'You have been obedient but not willing.'

The lord threw the book at him, took him to the book. Hagin found that it is easy to make an adjustment to your spirit, more so when your theology has been upended! He got 'willing pretty fast,' as he was to say several times. He frantically declared this to the Lord and the Devil. The Lord authenticated the new position. He was not done with him though.

'You do not practice what you preach,' the Lord reproved. Hagin cringed and told the Lord he had dealt him a low blow there. In spite of his protests the Lord insisted that Hagin was lopsided in the sense that he believed God for healing but not for finances. The same principles of faith he practiced in healing could be generalized to finances. Faith worked in every realm whether it be healing, salvation, marital, finances, baptism and what have you. It was a staggering revelation. A truth lost to the church in plain sight had been unearthed.

The Lord though was not done yet. KEH had been so indoctrinated by the religious small town piety and filthy lucre position, the Lord saw it fit to straighten his theology. The Lord took him back to the book of the beginnings (Genesis). The Lord explained to Brother Hagin that it was him, the Lord who had made the world and its fullness thereof (Psalms 89:11) He had made it all for his man Adam. The tenth verse of Psalms 50 states that '***every beast of the forest is mine, and the cattle upon a thousand hills {v.10}***. Haggai 2:8 expressly says '***the silver and gold are the Lord's*** ' Haggai 2:8'. The lord was the creator, and the owner but he turned over the title to his beloved Adam. The cattle upon a thousand hills, the jaguars and Rolls Royce upon a thousand highways, the gold and emeralds were not for the devil and his crowd. They were for his man Adam. Adam's stewardship was faulty. He was the de facto god of the earth, made to rule and dominate the world but he committed high treason and surrendered his dominion to the enemy.

What a sell out!

Ignorance costs the earth!

Remember this is January 1950 when the Lord was dealing with KEH along these lines. By selling out Adam traded places with the adversary. Satan became the god of the earth as so aptly identified by 2nd Corinthians 4:4. It was not the Lord who was withholding the essentials from his family: it was the hand of the enemy. Culpability lay with the devil, the god of the world. He proceeded to tell Reverend Hagin that money was down there on earth. The Lord had no greenbacks

(US Dollars) in heaven. If he was to rain US bills these would be counterfeits. Silver and gold were down on earth. It was the devil preventing money from coming in. All KEH had to do was to say 'I claim an x amount of money, devil get your hand off my money, go ministering angels, cause the money to come. '[see What God Taught Me About Prosperity].

Now that he had found this truth, KEH sought to prove this theory.

He cancelled a meeting at a relatively large church and went right out into the country side, to a small village. He had preached there before and they had paid him $114.30 for two weeks. It was just a small group. KEH told the Lord that he was claiming $150.00 that week. He said it on the basis that you can have whatever you say.

Much to the host Pastor's chagrin Pastor Hagins advised him not to make a pull for the money and simply state that this is an offering for brother Hagin and pass the plate. No overzealous fundraising gimmicks. The Host pastor, went along with Pastor Higgins' plan but felt that this itinerant Evangelist would not get a quarter at that rate. The Pastor asked him to stay until the following Wednesday. Brother Hagin went back to the Lord and adjusted the figure to $200- up from $150-. Then Wednesday night came. It was time to collect an offering for the travelling Evangelist. The host pastor, in a mundane fashion, novel to him though, collected the offering without much fanfare. The sum collected took him aback: 240 dollars and 15 cents. He said he had never seen anything like that.

'Wherein the world is the money coming from?' He exclaimed.

Ephesians says he is able to do more exceedingly abundantly than we can ask or think. The Lord had 'out done' Brother Hagin, by $40, 15.

Reverend Hagin began to purposefully target small country churches, to prove the Word of God. The results left the hosts shell shocked. A deluge of money overwhelmed him. His faith grew. Whereas in 1950, it took all the faith he had to raise $150-, 30 years later he could believe God for a million dollars with relative ease.

Life in the field was not easy. In his tape *Saying for your Finances (Mountain Moving Faith Series*), he recounts a story when he was driving home just before Christmas from another meeting where the offering fell way below the mark. Due to the state of the tyres he had to travel at mid night, when the roads were cooler. On his way home, doubt and worry over Christmas began to creep in. The back wheel began to make a sound which seemed to musically ask 'what you gonna do, what are you gonna do--?'

How excruciating!

Soon another tyre joined and the duet went 'What you gonna do---?' The third tyre joined in to make a trio and soon a quartet of tired tires were singing tirelessly,

'What you gonna do?'

KEH shouted back at the tires 'I will tell you what I am gonna do, I am going to believe the bible means what it says and I don't have a single worry in the world.'

He got home to a worried Oretha.

'Do you have a meeting lined up?' she asked anxiously.

Kenneth told her not to worry about a thing in the world. It was in the hands of the Lord to set things up for him for the benefit of all. He went straight to bed. Soon a call came through. Ever motherly Oretha began to protectively shield her tired husband from the phone call. Reverend Hagin asked her to bring the handset. It was a pastor from another Church. The conversation went something like this. The Pastor said 'Brother Hagin you don't know me, Can you hold a service for me?'

'Sure I can,'

'When can you start?'

'Tomorrow'

His name is Jehovah Jireh: the lord is our provider. Folks who don't live by faith, they sure miss out a lot, they sure miss out a lot, he said contemplatively.

WAITING ON THE LORD AND NEW HORIZONS OF REVELATION.

Oral Roberts and Kenneth E Hagin's teachings were revolutionary and revelatory. In the fifties Oral Roberts shocked both the circular and Christian world when he proclaimed that God is a good God! Like KEH and others he upended many a folks theology when he talked about Jesus healing in this day and age, and told people to expect a miracle. It was revolutionary and sparked controversy. KEH and Oral Roberts were accused of preaching a cheap and easy gospel. Most Christians those days believed in a harsh and judgmental God of does and don'ts. Like Moses's rod swallowing Pharaoh's magicians' rod, his God given revelation prevailed. His critics went the way of Smith Wigglesworth's critics: they are long gone and forgotten but KEH and Oral Roberts' powerful words continue to move the hearts of multitudes across the globe.

The origins of KEH's teachings were eclectic, to say the least.

Divine revelation comes in many ways. The essence of it is that God, in his grace and from the abundance of his glorious treasury will lead you to some truth and graciously allow you to enter into experiences from which you will come out nourished, and insightful.

KEH was to say, he learnt about faith by reading his Grandmother's bible. Being Baptist the message of faith, more so on healing was not known to him. Still, the Lord gave him a breakthrough and he was healed by acting on Mark 11 vs. 23. He had maximised bible reading while bedridden and after being born again. When the Lord raised him from the bed, he proceeded to read more on faith and practice faith. He prayed for his Sunday School Master and he was healed. For a man who was to be used by the Lord to start a leading bible school, he only 'almost went' to a bible seminary. He shunned the idea of going to the denominational seminary because their teachings were bereft of the Holy Spirit, tongues and faith. Some seminaries can easily become cemeteries.

He read as many books as he could. Oretha remembers him, in those stormy early field ministry days, driving away with a suitcase full of books. Her son Kenneth W. Hagin also attests to this fact. He remembers his Father as studious in the last church he pastored before going out in ministry. Ken, then six to seven years old remembers his father, a 31 year old skinny tall young man sitting bowed over the desk. He would be studying the scriptures using the light from the little lamp on the desk. He would wake up in the night to find his father still be sitting on the same desk. The young father would make an open cast mine of scriptural gems. In the morning as they sat down for breakfast, his father would be on the desk, with the bible and several books strewn over the table, lying open with some spread all over the floor.

The young Pastor would invariably join the family at the breakfast table. On coming back from school, young Ken would find his father still slouched forward on the desk. There were many a times, when young Ken would wake up to find his father having prayed all night. He would then shower , clean up and set off on church's business without sleeping. The Holy Spirit would refresh him, he would reason. Kenneth W Hagin sums up by saying that his father got his revelation by studying the bible and good books, and by praying for hours on end.

'So if you have ever wondered how Kenneth E Hagin learned all that he knew and that he taught to many people over his almost 70 years of ministry, now you know. He received the revelation knowledge by studying the bible and other good books and by praying for hours on end.' (Hagin 2007:vi)

To get to where KEH was on his spiritual walk one has to be willing to pay the price.

KEH found that by praying in tongues for a prolonged time, the Holy Spirit would prepare him for things to come. He would a countless time, give an account of the way the Lord told him about the forthcoming healing revival. This was during an extended period of seeking God's face. He decided to pray for an hour but the devil laughed in his face and dared him to pray longer. He then doubled the times and launched further into four hours. Then in the fifth hour he hit the gusher, as he put it. A strong anointing of the Holy Spirit came upon him. Some folks, he observed, never pray long enough to hit the gusher. The revelation began to come. Revelation of things to come. The lord then told him about the coming healing revival at the close of the Second World War. He was praying in his study in Greggton, Texas 1943. He wrote the prophecy down. A year and a half later, in September 1944, he was preaching at a Pentecostal youth rally in East Texas. In the middle of the sermon, he read out what the Lord had revealed to him, and the power of God fell on the crowd. Everyone hit the floor and prayed in tongues. The revival of divine healing began in 1947. For all its power, the revival produced a lot of healing evangelists who did not have a sound grounding in the word and who were prone to some unscrupulous practices. KEH was heard, to say that long after most of these Evangelists are gone, he will still be standing. Only Oral Roberts and Brother Hagin appeared to have gone from strength to strength in the aftermath of the Healing Revival.

William Branham, during the healing revival was peerless and unparalleled in terms of the gift of knowledge , healing, miracles and the prophetic Ministry. With time though he fell out with his trusted management team which had helped him focus on his call to preach salvation, heal the sick and function in the prophetic office. He wandered into teaching, bringing up subjects he had a shaky grasp of. His doctrine became rickety, with the attendant problem of mutilating the scriptures. He thought he, William Branham was the seventh Angel, the last prophet and Elijah reincarnated. The seven letters in his first and last names bore witness to that, he would contend. He generated some not so theologically sound positions like every time there is 'a funeral it's a woman's fault, thanks to Eve.'

KEH who was also rising as a Prophet, preached at a Voice of Healing convention organised by Gordon Lindsay, Branham's former manager. After the meeting Gordon Lindsay asked Kenneth E Hagin to take a break and get something to eat. Brother Hagin said he could not eat, he had an urge to pray, and to pray urgently and fervently, a sudden and inexplicable burden to pray. Lindsay, KEH and others went with him to his hotel to pray. The word of the Lord came, saying the Lord was going to shortly remove the prophet in the land from their midst, for the saving of his soul and the body of Christ. The Prophet was misleading people with false doctrines.

By the 1960's William Branham had become an extremely controversial minister of the word. He had strayed from his office of evangelist/prophet and made a foray into teaching. In 1963 he identified himself as the eschatological prophet mentioned as the end time messenger, the seventh Angel of the Seventh Church Age, the final closing days of time. He, Branham was the last Prophet who had come in the spirit of Elijah to make way for the second coming of Christ. Reverend Hagin and Gordon Lindsay, after the prophetic word, at first thought that the prophecy was meant for Oral Roberts. It then dawned on them that it could not be Oral Roberts the Lord wanted to remove: Oral Roberts was an evangelist and not a prophet. They settled on Branham and after much prayer, Lindsay sought diligently to warn Branham about the impending danger. Branham now cold and distant towards Gordon Lindsay, refused to avail himself. Lindsay knew then that the prophecy was now irreversible.

On the 18th of December 1965, William Branham who had been holidaying in Tucson, Arizona came back to Jefferson, Indiana. Three miles east of Friona, Texas, a drunk driver traveling west, in the eastbound lane missed the car which was being driven by Branham's son and hit Branham's car head on. Branham died on the spot.

A prolonged season of prayer in the spirit synchronises us with what the Lord is doing and is going to do. Spend time seeking God's face.

CHAPTER FIVE: Praying in the Spirit and Charting the Course of One's Life.

KEH recounts the time when he was a single young preacher bereft of a helpmate. He was praying in tongues when he got the revelation of being married. He had an inward revelation that he would be married, and would have two children, first a boy and then a girl. Much to his family's chagrin he began telling them he will have a boy first. He was however not working on 'supposings'. He was standing on certainty.

God's word is deterministic and not probabilistic.

He was not married then. Things turned out to be exactly as he had foretold. This was to be a frequent occurrence in his life. He said,

'The Holy Spirit would reveal different steps in God's plan for my life and ministry as I took time to pray in the Spirit and fellowship with the Father.' Some people are looking for something they can do to achieve success. The answer does not lie in one's natural strength and reasoning faculties. It lies in waiting on God, spending hours praying in the Holy Ghost.' That is how he got direction and revelation for every step and stage of his ministry.

Oral Roberts remembered a time when he was still a full time pastor in Enid and also attending University. The Lord spoke to him clearly,
'Son, don't be like other men. Don't be like any denomination. Be Like Jesus and heal his people as he did.'
The Lord's word shook him to the very core of his being. He asked the Lord how he was going to know how to heal people and to be like Jesus. The Lord told him to read the four gospel

and the book of acts three times consecutively while on his knees within thirty days. Oral Roberts began a season of fasting and praying as he soaked in the word. He became acutely aware of his weakness and impotence. Remember the friend's cry,

'I have nothing to set before him!'

He knew that in his weakness the strength of the Lord was made perfect (2 Cor 12:9). He would go on in later years to describe the prayerful reading of the five books as a pivotal moment in his ministry. Jesus and his healing power became real to him. He saw that our Lord Jesus did three things on earth: preach, teach and heal. The person of Jesus became real to him. After the thirty days were over he threw himself to the floor and told the Lord he was not going to get up until the Lord revealed himself to him. He sought the Lord with everything that was in him. He poured himself out like water for a long time. Then the voice of the Lord came. The Lord told him to get up; get into his car and drive east. Oral Roberts did as he was told, hollering all the time. Then the Lord said to him,

'From this hour you shall have my power to heal the sick and cast out demons.'

KEH stated that he and Oral Roberts had great respect for one another. The pair spent many times in fellowship together. He noted how Oral Roberts knew how to pray [Tongues- Beyond the Upper Room.] Oral Roberts knew how to enter into the presence of the Lord. KEH knew this because they had prayed together several times and been in the presence of the Lord together. They discussed different subjects together. On tongues they discovered they had a great deal in common. When they compared notes they discovered that the pattern of their ministries had been unveiled to them in exactly the same way : waiting upon the Lord; speaking in tongues and interpreting them. This had given the direction/trajectory their ministries took over the years. These principles apply to one's career, studies, business pursuits, marital life and what have you!

KEH marveled at a remark made by a Pastor at one Full Gospel Business Men Fellowship meeting,

'Brother Hagin, a few years ago no one had ever heard of you but now, no one has not heard of you!' That just about sums it all up.

The origin of Kenneth E Hagin's success has generated a lot of debate. More so for a preacher who went through two revivals (healing and then charismatic renewal revival) before bursting onto the national scene and be the foremost leader of the 'World Church', in the process spearheading the teaching revival, and is recognized as the father of the **Word of Faith Movement**.

Oral Roberts was no doubt another man who found good success in the Lord.

Oral Roberts explained his secrets to success in his book *When You See The INVISIBLE, You Can Do The IMPOSSIBLE.* He laments the hit and miss approach to pursuits in the first 12 years of his ministry. Decision making was a random process. He didn't put himself in a position where he could make a decision jointly with the Lord. Similarly he did not seek divine guidance in pursuit of a project which needed God's go ahead or advice. He says this made him spiritually wobbly. He could not venture into a huge undertaking with the inner assurance that God was in it. He had no pattern for life. 'I could make no definite decisions nor attempt great things with any degree of confidence that God was in them.'

Very creative and ever bubbling with energy, Oral Roberts was haunted by the fact that he could not strike out in any direction with a knowing in his heart that there will be fruition at the end of the tunnel. He knew he could not continue that way, living in an unsettled state. How did people like Paul make God ordered decisions and set to achieve the Holy Spirit commissioned missions or projects? He studied the gifts of the Holy Spirit as laid down in 1 Corinthians 12. He was fascinated by the revelation gifts such as the word of knowledge and the discernment of spirits. He was drawn to the interpretation of tongues and the gifts of tongues, but struggled to understand them in a practical way. The Lord gave him grace in 1963, and he was able to talk to the Lord at will about the things of the Lord and interpret back to himself what the Lord would have said to him. Direction, divine guidance burst forth.

'The Holy Spirit personalises what God is saying to you in his word. To me that has been very important.'

This, to me, is another form of Rhema- the spoken word of the Lord.

Way back in 1935, the Lord had told him to build him a University established on the authority of the Holy Ghost. The know how eluded him. When the time came as his healing ministry raced to its climax he found himself facing the gargantuan task of tackling the knowledge deficit. He would stare at the building site and feel lost. He had no money, no faculty, no know how and was bereft of people who believed that he could do it. But the Lord had commanded him. Suddenly tongues swirled up from deep inside him like a whirlpool. After interpreting them in the human language he knew exactly how to go about building the university.

Another thing he also said he would do when facing a project is to 'plant a seed'. In fact a life/rhythm of sowing and reaping was his. Over the years, together with his wife Evelyn, they had accumulated a small estate/equity. They sold the estate and gave it over to the ministry as seed-faith to start the work of the university. The work took off. The University was built. Oral Roberts said when God calls you he will never let you down. He will equip you and back you to the hilt even if it doesn't't look like that at first.

These two principles, interpretation of tongues and sowing a seed became his sesame for success (so to speak) in human terms.

How does this then compare to Kenneth E Hagin's revelation for success in both one's personal success and ministry? No doubt both men's approaches when reduced to their atoms were

1) If the Lord does not build a house, the builders build in vain. What has God told you? What does God want you to do with your life? God's plan and purposes as revealed to an individual are the essence of success. If the Lord is not in it and you are on your own, you have an uphill task to get 'good success.'
2) You must be led by the Lord. The Lord has different ways of leading people- giving revelational knowledge. For Oral Roberts it was mainly the interpretation of tongues. There is no doubt that KEH got many a revelation speaking in tongues, but he discussed a broader platform in terms of the leadings of God. Visions, one's inner spirit, and the voice of the Holy Spirit were vehicles the Lord used to unveil his plan.

KEH said ' In the 1987 visitation of the Lord, Jesus told me that-------------if the body of Christ cooperate with God and get in line with his plan, purposes and pursue that plan God will accomplish what he wants to------.'[See his book *Plans, Purposes and Purs*uits.]

God accomplishing what he wants through us is essentially the very fabric of our achieving success. Failure to capture the vision, and failure to be in the lord's perfect will, will just plunge us into oblivion, laboring fruitlessly to the point of mediocrity, frustration and bitterness and bickering and even premature physical death.

In his book ***Plans, Purposes and Pursuits*** (PPP) he talks about the 1987 visitation. He says he was caught up with the Lord Jesus and he began to see how men devise their own plans. The plans maybe good and even scriptural, but far from God's plans for them! Build according jto God's pattern. Hebrews 8:5

----as Moses was admonished of God when he was about to make the tabernacle: for, See, saith he, that thou make all things according to the pattern shewed to thee in the mount.

He says 'the reason people fail and the reason ministries fail is because they have the wrong plan, purpose, and motive.'

Whatever the Christian is doing he must ask himself 'is this God's plan?'

See to it that you build according to the pattern given to you!

He says it 'pays in every way to wait before Him and get his plan.'

He noted that so many times people devise their plans and then ask the Lord to bless the plans. The plan of the Lord however, comes blessed already.

One needs to stir one's self to discover God's plan for this life and ministry.

KEH remembers his restlessness when he was pastoring a church. Something was wrong but he could not put a finger on it. He told the Lord there was something wrong. He felt like he was washing with his socks on. He began to pray and seek God's face. He was already a man of prayer but carrying this extra burden made him spend more time in prayer.

He agonised before the Lord. Why he was not satisfied, yet he was pastoring the best church he had ever pastored? His income was the best he had ever had. He was living in the best parsonage he had ever lived in. Why then was he restless? What was amiss?

The Lord was unequivocally blunt.

'What is wrong with you is that I never called you to pastor to begin with. This is not your calling.'

His 12 years as a Pastor were not in God's perfect will. They were simply in God's permissive will. The Lord had graciously allowed him to continue in that vein. Pastoring however was not his calling. KEH, did not however take time to ask the Lord what it is he wanted him to do. He fell into the denominational error when it was time to go in the field and set off as an itinerant evangelist. In his own words

'I fell flat on my face.' He would say in his book Plans, Purposes and Pursuits.

After a year as an Evangelist, he had worn out his car and sold it for junk. They lived in a not so commodious 3 room apartment. Young Kenneth Jnr had to sleep in a rollaway bed in winter and on a 'screened -in back porch' in the summer. The children were not adequately provided for. Once again he sought the Lord. Again, he felt that he was washing his feet with his socks on. He sensed that the Lord wanted to bring him to a place where he could follow the plan of the God. The Lord wanted him to fulfil his commission to teach. According to Ephesians 4:11, 12 the Lord gave people various gifts: some apostles; and some, prophets; and some, evangelists, and some, pastors and teachers;

In those days everyone called to a powerful ministry was a preacher/evangelist, had a tent and modelled himself along the lines of Charles Price or later on William Branham. He had jumped on the **Evangelist** bandwagon, when his true calling was that of a **Teacher.** In one's personal life and indeed in one's ministry it is of fundamental importance to take time in prayer and find out God's will for one's life specifically. KEH observed that the Lord wants us to move not only in his plans for our lives but in the plan for the body of Christ here on earth. KEH knew that the mantle for teaching had dropped on him, and he had been called to the ministry of teaching. In the 1949/1950 though, the people wanted preachers and not teachers. He had subconsciously fashioned his plans according to the thinking of man. The Lord would not have it any other way than his way. KEH sought the Lord, fully aware that he needed to walk in the light of the Lord's plan. And that's how you get his full blessings.

Still locked in the prolonged period of seeking God's face, he conducted a meeting in Henderson, Texas. The meeting ran from the last Sunday of 1949 right through to January 1950. During the meeting he told the Lord that he was going to teach on a Friday and the Lord was going to see the folly of him teaching. So far the meeting had been going on for a week, with no one having been born again, and no one had been filled with the spirit. Only one little girl had lifted her hand up for prayer. On that Friday night he taught on the subject of faith. After teaching for 45 minutes he made an alter call, even though he thought no one will come up. Five grownups responded to the alter call and gave their lives to the Lord. KEH says

'I hadn't been able to sleep for praying, but after that I wasn't able to sleep for repenting!'

By obediently following God's plan, four new families were added to the church in that service. In those days, in Pentecostal circles it was a landslide to get six people saved and two people filled with the Holy Spirit in a three week revival. He started to teach. He knew that God's plan was for him to teach and to stand in the office of a Prophet. He went to another church and 12 new families were added to the church. This became a common occurrence wherever he went. The secret being that he was now diligently following God's plan and God's purposes. It is no good following church traditions. One needs to hear from heaven for himself! KEH warned against simply following programs and pursuits which belong to other people. What if it's not God's plan for you?

One needs to go down on his knees and find out what God's plan is. God puts his blessings on the plans which meet his approval. God's plan is fruitful, abounding in overwhelming results. I have found that when I am in God's plan astounding miracles happen and doors open.

Psalms 127:1

Except the Lord build the house, they labour in vain that build it------.

If you are out of God's plan, you will labour and struggle, but it will all be in vain. If you are a Pastor, you need to spend time seeking God's face, waiting on him. That way you become sensitive to the Holy Spirit and know God's will. Some preachers, according to KEH wouldn't know the Holy Spirit if he comes down the street with a red hat on. They will continue with their little programs in a service even if the Holy Spirit has a different plan at that moment. They find they are being left out. You must get God's best!

KEH cites Psalms 127:1 as his mainstay in decision making. He said he never made a move unless he knew that God was in it. His staff would at times get frustrated as he delayed coming up with an answer while he sought God's guidance over an issue. Your plans may fail, but God's plans never fail. Sometimes one can be led astray by things which look legitimate and good. If however the Lord is not in them then you forfeit the fullness of God's blessing. On the 1st of October 1979, Kenneth E Hagin started the healing school on the RHEMA campus. The first 45 minutes were spent on singing, worshipping and praising the Lord. The Lord then reminded KEH that the meeting was not a worship meeting. It was a healing meeting. They only had to sing to get people into the swing of things and then go straight into the teaching of the Word of God on healing. Similarly a lot of time was being consumed on counselling in the Healing and Prayer Centre. They had even built rooms for counselling in the Centre. The Lord told him that he had not told him to counsel. Folks should only get counselling in their own sheepfold. He, KEH could only counsel those who were of his own sheepfold like students, staffers and so forth. The shepherd lives with the sheep, and that is the role of the Pastor. KEH always encouraged people to send their tithes to their churches. They could send him offering, but they needed to support their local church through tithe.

KEH also followed God's plan by having to change his plans. The Lord had given him his plan and purpose: they began to hold faith seminars and indoor camp meetings. Then they unconsciously slid from the original plan of camp-meeting three years down the line. One day KEH was praying at three am when the Lord spoke to him. The Lord reminded him that mornings were supposed to be for the faith seminar, afternoon for the Holy Spirit sessions and evening times for the Camp meeting preaching. They had somehow changed the format and had all sorts of topics being delivered by different preachers. Working intimately with the Lord was his secret for success.

'See to it that you build to the pattern given to you by the Lord........'

KEH talked about a Pastor who flew all over the USA following successful Pastors and trying to find out and copy their plans. He was not making any progress though. He asked KEH for a plan. KEH, advised him to go on his knees and find out what God's plan was for his life! The Pastor said that he had no time to pray: he was too busy to find out God's plan!

At one point KEH attended an 'Idea Exchange,' meeting. Many Ministers from various denominations attended. Some of the ministers approached KEH and asked him,

'When I first knew you, nobody had ever heard of you. You were preaching in small churches and, once in a while, in a large church. But then, all of a sudden, you became not only a national figure, but in just a matter of years – an international figure.......what is your secret of success?'

KEH answered

'The only secret of success I know is walking in line with the word of God, and praying and listening to the Holy Spirit.'

He said 'Actually everything I am doing today is the result of believing the word, praying in tongues and being obedient to what God has told me to do.'

Like Oral Roberts he would say 'thank God for the value of praying in tongues....praying in tongues was instrumental in even showing me about my marriage and my children.'

Earlier on, I recounted KEHs' praying in a barn loft that belonged to one of his deacons. He had been going out with Oretha for some time now. He began to 'pray out' his future in tongues. Then he interpreted the tongues. He saw then in the spirit that he was going to marry Oretha and have two children. That came to pass. He raised his mother's ire by naming the unborn first child Ken. What if it turns out to be a girl? It turned out to be a boy. As he had been told by Heaven, it came to pass. This did not come to pass because he was standing in the office of a prophet. It came to pass because he sought God's plan for his life. He would exhort: get God's plan and it will work like clockwork.

You have to learn to wait on God. You don't fall to your knees and rise quickly without the inner assurance that the battle is won. It's about running the race with patience. Once he was driving a Minister friend around the Rhema campus. The Minister friend saw the gigantic campus and the vast faculties. He remarked that KEH must be facing a mammoth task running such a gargantuan ministry. KEH replied that he was carrying no burden. He had never intended to do all this. The Lord had led him to it. It was for the Lord to finish.

It is important to find your place of anointing. Its folly to try to be a jack of all trades and a master of none. If you find your place you will be successful. KEH cites the case of D.R and Mrs. Howard Carter who found the first Pentecostal Bible School in the world. Mr. Carter had twelve years of college education and spoke 32 languages fluently. They were mightily gifted in the gifts of the Holy Spirit. KEH heard D.R Carter say once that practically everyone he laid hands on received the Holy Spirit and spoke in tongues and practically everyone his wife laid hands on was healed. Know your place.

At other times, you might correctly catch the vision, know what God wants you to do. Still, many a folks miss it by not understanding the timing of the vision. You must wait for the quickening of the Spirit. He explores this topic in the book ***Fulfilling God's Plan For Your Life*** {FGPYL}

Everyone has a race to run- a place in the anointing, but you must run with patience. Insight into the timing of God's plan is essential. 1 Chronicles 12:32

And of the children of Issachar, which were men that had understanding of the times, to know what Israel ought to do------

The sons of Isaachar were named among the valiant men who stood by David. David's great men had slain giants and lions and did incredible feats. The Lord was mighty in the sons of Isaachar to reveal the future.

The last part of Hebrews 12:1 says ***WITH PATIENCE let us run the race that is set before us.***

God's timing is perfect. You need to understand it, to develop a discerning heart. KEH pointed out that a Christian, can hinder the race by not having patience. The race is to be run with patience. Just because the Lord has given you a plan does not mean you have to do it immediately. People tend to muddy the water by jumping ahead of the Lord. KEH said,

'As I grew in the Lord, I learned not to jump out ahead of Him, but just to allow Him to bring to pass His purposes , but just to allow Him to bring to pass His purposes for me as a I stayed faithful to prepare myself.'[FGPYL].

Time spent in preparation is not time and is never time wasted. It calls for sacrifice but in the end it will pay.

It was for the Christian to know the 'what' of the Lord's plan, and it was for the Lord to know the 'how and when' of the plan. Waiting upon the Lord in prayer gives you a real time alignment with God's will and very current plan.

The Lord takes you step by step. You may not be ready for the next step and the Lord takes his time, preparing you. Be patient. Rest in the Lord. Wait upon the Lord in prayer.

Be still and know that God is God.

'God has a way, but he also has a timing.' Reverend Hagin reflected [FGYPYL].

It is important to remember that the timing of the Lord is perfect.

It is important to remember that God's time is the right time.

Moses sensed God calling him along the lines of delivering the children of Israel. The problem was that he wanted to do it in his time, with his strength and in his own way. His haste might have actually delayed God's plan! At the age of 40 he killed an Egyptian who was ill-treating a Hebrew slave. That was not what God had planned for Israel! Moses had to run away from the wrath of Pharaoh. It was after forty years that he emerged from the wilderness with God's OWN plan of deliverance [FGPFYL]. Ironically 4, 40, 8, 80 are digits used in pivotal events or watershed years. It could be that at 40 God was ready to use Moses, but Moses got in the way with his misdirected zeal! Emancipation for him was more political

than spiritual!
To be like the sons of Isaachar, to develop spiritual sensitivity one must spend time in prayer.
Acts 13:2 says
'As they ministered to the Lord, and fasted, the Holy Ghost said, Separate me Barnabas and Saul for the work whereunto I have called them.'

As they ministered unto the Lord, direction came.
When the Holy spirit told Reverend Hagin to start the bible school and later on the healing school, a lot of other people wrote to him saying that they felt that the Lord wanted them to do that as well, but did not know how to. KEH would tell them that if God wanted them to do that he was going to show them how to do it. Bit by bit his plan, the Lord will unveil, and all you have to do is follow. Some try to use their strength and fail to trust God to unveil the plan in HIS own time and bring his plan to pass. 'If you are labouring by yourself, you might burn out. You need to rest in his glory and strength.' KEH said. Hebrews 4:3 says '...we which have believed do enter into rest......'

CONSECRATION

Obedience, as a theme runs through Oretha's book. KEH ends his book Plans, Purposes and Pursuits with a prayer along the lines of obedience. Moved by the spirit of the Lord KEH made this prayer at the 'Homecoming '87.' He prayed that Christians be willing to pay the price for walking in God's plan. There is a price one has to pay. He prayed that the Lord would forgive the saints who have failed to enter into the things of the Lord, because they thought the price was too big to pay. We hold back and lose out. The lord shows us things and we hold back. The Lord needs to help us dedicate ourselves and consecrate ourselves day and night to do his will so that his plan is fulfilled. We are to have no plan but the Lord's bidding, and his plans. There is a move of the Spirit coming, but we need to avail ourselves to the Lord. Consecration is the turning point for us to step into the great move of God. We need to pay the full price. God's way is the best. The natural mind, will not understand these things and we must not let it rob us of God's best. ***We must soak ourselves in prayer.*** Many are the ones God is calling. If they prove to be faithful, they will be promoted to a greater anointing.

'A stronger anointing will come upon them and it will be increased greatly. And they'll move into a higher place of ministry for there .....are different measures, different dimensions in the same office.'

'For those things he has prepared for us, the Lord may he prepare us for them. Consecration is not just for the night, the week or the year or next year, consecration is forever.'

'O Lord with You I will go.' He pledges in the prophetic prayer [PPP].

LEADINGS

For a mighty Prophet of God like Kenneth E Hagin one would have expected him, humanly speaking to emphasize visions and dreams. Yet, when it comes to divine guidance, in both our daily lives and /pursuing God's plans for our lives, he devoted the bulk of his time on teaching the body of Christ to know how to be led by the inner man, the inner witness or your spirit- all being variant terms for being led from 'inside' [see ***How You Can Know the Will of God***].

Waiting on the Lord in prayer is key to getting to know God's mind and his plan for your life. A lot of people don't take time to wait for the Lord and don't take responsibility for knowing which way the Lord wants them go. KEH points out that some will simply tell the Lord to open the door if it is his will, if it is not his will then let him shut the door. Obviously, it is easier to go down that route than to take time before the Lord until the inner witness has come. The inner witness is drowned out by the daily activities of life, things we busy ourselves with in the physical and mental realm. The things of the spirit become indistinct and somewhat incoherent. One needs to learn to quieten the mind and hear the voice of his regenerated spirit as the spirit hears from the Spirit of the Lord. Too many of us have educated our minds at the expense of our spirits. The result is that 'there are a thousand and one things we would never have done if we had listened to that inner witness,' Reverend Hagin was wont to say.

We have invested money where we shouldn't have and have lost the money instead. We have partnered with people we should not have partnered with and saw our ventures hit the rock. We have made disastrous career choices and moves, because we crowded the inner witness out. We preferred to hear the voice of man and not God's voice. Of the inner witness KEH said when one is praying along certain lines and contemplating on the word of God, there might come to him a check, 'on the inside', telling him not to do something. Similarly, there might come a leading, urging him to do something or giving him a green light on an issue under consideration. This will be the inward witness in operation. Sometimes one has to wait a while to get it. You need to quieten the mind when you go before the Lord. The mind tends to wander about when one is in prayer. KEH used to need at least an hour to quieten his mind when waiting before the Lord. He however discovered that speaking in tongues kept his spirit focused on God and his mind quiet.

In some cases the Lord will lay something in your heart even while you are walking and you suddenly know what will happen and what you ought to do. Paul, in a dangerous voyage in a Rome bound ship said in Acts 27 v.10 says these words,

*'........ **Sirs, I perceive that this journey will be with hurt and much damage, not only of the lading and ship, but also of our lives.'***

Paul here did not say the Lord told him. He said he perceived. He had sensed in his spirit.

There is no doubt that knowing God's will and getting divine guidance is a covenant promise. Colossians 1 vs. 9-10 says 'for ***this cause, we also since the day we heard it, do not cease to pray for you, and to desire that you might be filled with the knowledge of his will in all wisdom and spiritual understanding; That ye might walk worthy of the Lord unto all pleasing, being fruitful in every good work and increasing in the knowledge of the God.***'

Be filled with knowledge of his will in all wisdom and spiritual understanding!

In pursuing good success in the ministry KEH, like Billy Graham lived a humble and modest life, free from the fetters of flamboyance, worldly pursuits, politics and cheap politicking. Billy Graham though did dabble in politics now and again but mainly from an idealist position and not from being a regime change fanatic.

Like an Athlete in the hunt for a prize, don't be weighed down by the dead matters of this life!

Hebrews 12:1 is particularly instructive on this score.

Wherefore seeing we also are compassed about with so great a cloud of witnesses, let us lay aside every weight, and the sin which so easily beset us, and let us RUN with patience the RACE that is set before us.

Lay aside every weight including the prima facie legitimate ones. The early Apostles noticed that getting entangled with the daily distribution of food was encroaching on their prayer lives.

Acts 6:3, 4 says

Wherefore, brethren, look ye out among you seven

men of honest report-------whom we might appoint over this business------but we give ourselves to prayer, and to the ministry of word.

We must also lay aside any weights which hinder us from following God's plan. These might be sin, spiritual slothfulness, fear, double mindedness, self-ambition, our own inclinations and so forth. It might not be sin, but things that are good in themselves, yet still they will be things which the Lord did not plan for us and can mislead us. It may be legitimate pursuits which you might become engrossed in but you will be doing them out of self-ambition and own motives rather than to advance the Kingdom of God. Wigglesworth said anything that takes you out of the will of God is lust and when lust is fulfilled it brings death to your vision. One needs to follow God's plan to the letter and he will be exalted by the Lord to a summit where miracles abound [Wigglesworth: Greater Works than These].

Oral Roberts on of Interpretation of Tongues.

Oral Roberts and Kenneth E Hagin, two contemporaries, were in a deep conversation, when a stranger walked up to them and said 'I just want to shake hands with these great competitors'

They were not competitors.

They were co-laborers in the vineyard of the Lord.

Although at face value their positions on seed -faith giving appeared to differ, their positions and experiences on new depths of prayer were startlingly similar. Kenneth E Hagin remarked that nobody he ever knew, knew how to enter into the presence of the Lord in prayer like Oral Roberts. Brother Hagin knew this because he had prayed with Oral Roberts at times. He too had been up there several times in prayer and feared that he might not come back.

As noted earlier the two had compared notes on how their ministries' pattern of development and noted that that they had all obtained direction by speaking in tongues and asking the Lord for the interpretation.

.

They agreed that tongues are a formidable force for obtaining divine guidance.

We crave to hear from God but we waver on whether the Lord can really talk to us. Can he direct our path?

Can we get to know God's mind, in real time on the day to day issues we confront?

Oral Roberts' had agonized over this issue.

The Lord gave him a rather novel and powerful revelation of 1 Corinthians 14:13, 14,15

13 Wherefore let him that speaketh in an unknown tongue, pray that he may interpret.

14 if I pray in an unknown tongue my spirit prayeth but my understanding is unfruitful.

15 What is it then? I will pray with the spirit and I will pray with the understanding also---

Many a folk believe that to mean when we are filled with the Holy Spirit we should start to pray for God to give us the gift of interpretation of tongues. To a certain point they are right, but Oral Roberts' divinely granted revelation is interesting,

'My personal experience ....is this : when I finish praying in tongues—a few seconds or minutes----I pray for the interpretation........I ask God for it just as the Apostle Paul says in 1 Corinthians 14:13.' (Roberts 93:40.) He would pray in tongues and then he would then wait patiently for the Lord to give him an **understanding** of the tongues. He would then pray with both his spirit (speaking mysteries) and then pray with an understanding of the deep hidden things which the Lord would have fashioned and furnished for the hour. The message in season would have dawned on him. He won't be praying the 'problem' any more. No, he will be 'praying the mind of God' for the hour. That is powerful.

'The Lord has given me the tongue of the learned. To speak a word in season to him who is weary.'

Isaiah 50:4

Reduced to its atoms, asking for interpretation is asking for the mysteries to be revealed! You then pray in the power of the new revelation.

Divine direction then comes forth. Victory bursts in. Remember how Oral Robert described how he found the task of building a University based on God's authority daunting, mindboggling and even intimidating. He had just emerged from the healing ministry and was now on unchartered territory. The 'know how' was elusive. He however stood on that land where the University was to be built and prayed in tongues. The interpretation came forth. The Lord rolled out the know how before him. Suddenly he knew what to do. The building, the faculties, the students, and the modus operandi: they all flooded his consciousness and understanding. He saw the way to do it. The rest is history.

We all have a unique place in history. Speaking mysteries to the Lord, with understanding is a God given internal tracking system that keeps us in the perfect will of God. We will know what we ought to do in that particular hour.

Praying in the power of the Spirit, is described by Oral Roberts as God's Supernatural Tracking System (GSTS). In Psalms 18:33 the psalmist says

' He [the Lord God] maketh my feet like the hind's feet. And setteth me upon my high places.'

When sickness strikes you, it is the lowlands of your life you find yourself in. Not the high places. We are to be like the hind however, the female deer. It rides in high places. It perches itself on the high places, on the mountain top. O, the Lord, our father so very much desires to see us going higher and higher. Deuteronomy 26:19 says

'***and will make you high above all nations which he has made, in praise and in name, and in honour....***' AMP

Oral Roberts describes the deer as the 'most correlated' animal on planet earth (Roberts 1993:123.) It is supremely well coordinated. It has a special inbuilt tracking system. Oral

Roberts says ' Her back feet track so perfectly with her front feet that when she hits the ground with her front feet, her back feet follow in perfect unison, landing in exactly the same spot, without missing an inch.'

This is unique to the deer. She can scale a steep precipice, streak across a lowland; slice through the rocky side of the mountainside surefootedly and reach for the summit of the mountain with looseness and abandon. The horse may be strong, fast and imposing but it does not have the perfect tracking system which the deer has. On a deer hunt, Oral Roberts hired some horses to track the deer which were high up in the mountain. Halfway up the mountain, the horses stalled: they were afraid of falling. Their back feet missed the spot hit by the front feet by only 2-4 inches but this significantly raised the possibility of a fall. The deer had no such problems! The Lord, through praying in the spirit and understanding has given us the supernatural ability to ride upon the high places of our lives. To reach our potential. To be what the Lord wants us to be. To have God's best. To be high fliers. We can, with abandon run this race, scale the heights, skip over bulwarks and reach the height of our spiritual walk, ministry, family goals, career and business. We not to be at the bottom of the heap, Oral Roberts said. We are to be the head and ahead! You can only maintain your surefootedness and momentum if you get into the rhythm of praying in the spirit and praying with your understanding. There is a sermon which only you can preach. There is a book, a song and something which only you can come up with as foreordained by the Lord. To reach that height though, you need the surefootedness of the deer, the inbuilt tracking system which comes through praying in tongues and with your understanding. Hearing from God and following where the Lord leads. We are the pair of back feet, which must land where the Holy Spirit, the pair of the front feet, marks out. If we are not in sync with the Holy Ghost, we slip and tumble into oblivion or we get trapped in a cocoon of mediocrity. The deer's front feet are the Holy Ghost. We are the back feet. If we land where the Holy Spirit has pinpointed we won't stumble. We will not hurtle down into oblivion with a sickening thud. We will triumph and defy human wisdom. We will go against the odds. We will go higher and higher. The world will say how did he get up there in his ministry? We shall testify that the Lord in his goodness and mercy has directed us.

The way of the Lord is perfect.

2 Samuel 22:31 says

'As for God, his way is perfect; the word of the Lord is tried...'

Once I was praying in tongues and with my understanding. The Lord began to lead me to take urgent steps to sort out my driver's license. The Lord helped me to start driving in no time at all, and that boosted my income by more than twelve thousand dollars with even more far reaching implications social, marital and ministry wise.

Yes, he will set us upon our high places.

He makes us surefooted like the deer.

Going up meets resistance and dangers and high risks of slip ups. With the praying in the Holy Spirit, interpreting and following God's leading, we will like the deer ride upon our high places.

;

<u>The Holy Spirit as a Mighty River of Living Waters.</u>

John 7: 38 says

He that believeth on me, as the scripture hath said, out of his belly shall flow rivers of water. NKJV

Belly signifies the depth of your being. Words, and tongues do not originate from your tongue: they emerge from your belly and roll down your tongue. When the Holy Ghost flows out of your belly you are elevated into the realm of the miraculous. Speaking in tongues and interpreting catapults you into a victorious life.

Psalms 46:4 says

'There is a river whose streams shall make the glad the city of God.'

Is this gladness as in merry making or is this gladness due to victory, triumph and breakthrough? The latter is a more fitting when you look at vs.2

'Therefore we will not fear, Even though the earth be removed------.'

Praying in the power of the Holy Spirit releases the rivers of living water.

Living!

Giving life. Resuscitating. Reviving. Replenishing. Rejuvenating. Refreshing. Regenerating. O yes, resurrecting!

Ezekiel 47 comes to mind.

Vs. 1 says

Then he brought me back to the door of the temple; and there was water, flowing from under the threshold of the temple toward the east-----.'

The angel accompanying Ezekiel the prophet took him on a tour around the river of water. In verse three the water measured one thousand cubit and came up to his ankles. At two thousand cubic meters the water came to his knees, and at three thousand cubic meters the water was at his waist. At four thousand cubic meters the water was a mighty river and he could not walk, he had to swim. The digit four stands for fullness of time. The turning point. In Ezekiel's vision, at four thousand cubic meters the water was a fully blown mighty river. He had to flow with it. Children of God need to press on to new depths of Spirit filled prayer until they are flowing with the Holy Spirit. Walking and waddling is tantamount to limiting yourself to your own ability. Flow in the Spirit. Let your weight be borne by the Spirit. Let your direction be the direction of the Spirit. Let your pace be the pace of the Spirit.

'—water in which one must swim...'

Press into greater depths of Spirit filled prayer.

Depths where you are Holy Spirit bourne. The push, prompting and flow of the Holy Spirit move you on.

Vs. 8 Then he said to me: 'This water flows toward the eastern region, goes down into the village, and enters the sea. When it reaches, its waters are healed

Vs.9 and it shall be that every living that moves, wherever the rivers go, WILL LIVE. There will be a very great MULITITUDE OF FISH, because these WATERS GO THERE ----- NKJV.

The waters from the temple rushed towards the Dead Sea. At the tail end of verse 8 the amplified version says then they (

the living waters) ***go toward the sea, being made to flow into the sea and the waters of the dead sea shall be healed and become fresh***.

Because the dead sea has been healed all the creatures swarming in the path of the river will LIVE. Multitudes fish are now make home in the once dead sea. The stage is thus set for a mighty catch.

The Lord revealed to me that when we pray in the power of the Holy Ghost, with the mighty life giving river of the Holy Spirit flowing from our belly we give life to dead and deadening situations. At the time of that revelation, I was praying for a situation which at face value was manifestly hopeless. The country I was interceding for had been under the ruinous leadership of this dictator for decades. As I prayed in the spirit however, the river of water touched the hopeless situation and healed the situation. The Dictator was unexpectedly removed from office under mysterious circumstances. It was the hand of the Lord. The Holy Spirit also revealed to me that it is without wisdom that we write off a situation as hopeless. Romans 4 tells us that against hope in hope Abraham believed. Let the living river flow from your belly and change lives as you speak life to lifeless and dying lives, projects, churches, ministries and so forth. When the living rivers are flowing, it is time for your tongue to be weaponised and pull down strongholds and lift that which has fallen. When praying in the power of the Holy Spirit speak words of power.

Pastor Chris's take on speaking words of power is interesting

Romans 12:6

Having then gifts differing according to the grace that is given unto us, whether prophecy let us prophesy according to the proportion of faith.

There is a dichotomy between the faith utterance of a saint under the unction of the Holy Ghost and the revelation utterance of a prophet standing in the office of a prophet. In the former, a saint is moved by the Holy Ghost into FORTH-TELLING. In the later, the Prophet is moved into FORETELLING. The gift of forth telling is the gift of prophecy and Paul urges believers to have it in proportion to their faith. As a gift of the Holy Spirit the gift is given as the Spirit wills.

In the mouth of the Prophet, words of power come out

proclaim things that will happen in the future, that Word of the Lord comes to pass. Every believer can speak forth. Speak words of power to your situation. Don't speak despondency. Speak victory. Ezekiel 37 is instructive. It demonstrates the power of the spoken word when it has the full backing of the breath of the Lord behind it. The power of the Holy Ghost.

37 The hand of the Lord was upon me, and carried out me out in the spirit of Lord, and set me down in the midst of the valley which was full of bones'

2) [he] caused me to pass by then around about: and, behold there were very many in the open valley ; and, lo, they were very dry.

3) And he said unto me, Son of Man, can these bones live? And I answered, O Lord God, thou knowest.

Two key points jump out here.

Firstly, the situation was as hopeless as it could be. Not only were they disjointed bones strewn all over the valley in a haphazard fashion. They were very dry. The situation was impossibe. With God, however, nothing is impossible. He says in the book of Jeremiah

Behold I am the Lord, the God of all flesh, is there anything too hard for me?

Secondly, Ezekiel was being fatalistic. He was resigned to the state of affairs. He felt that it was out of his hands, he had no role to play!

'O Lord God, thou knowest.'

Ezekiel was keen to pass the responsibility of change to the Lord. The Lord showed him a better way. We are agents of change.

4] Again he said unto me, Prophesy upon these bones, and say unto them, O ye dry bones, hear the word of the Lord. Thus saith the Lord God unto these bones; I will cause breath to enter into you, and you shall live.

Having the breath of the Lord is tantamount to having the touch of the Holy Spirit

But if the same Spirit of him that raised up Jesus from the dead dwell[s] in you, he that raised up Christ from the dead shall also quicken your mortal bodies by his Spirit that dwelleth in you

Romans 8:11

And he prophesied.

As he prophesied the there was a dramatic turn -around of what had hitherto been an impossible situation.

V7. ***So I prophesied as I was commanded: and as I prophesied there was a noise, and behold a shaking, and the bones came together, bone to his bone.***

Behold a shaking........... The Holy Spirit is still in the business of shaking things up!

When they had prayed the place was shaken according to the the book of Acts jin chapter 4.

v8. ***And when I beheld, lo, the sinews and the flesh came upon them, and the skin covered above: but there was no breath in them.***

A miracle was underway but it was not complete. Thank God, he does not do half measures. We must not depart from our place of prayer until the miracle is complete! It is heartening to know that what he has started is a guarantee, an underwriting that he is willing and able to complete.

V9, prophesy, son of man, and say to the wind, thus saith the God; Come from the four winds, O breath, and breathe upon these slain, that they may live.

The wind is the Holy Spirit. The Holy Spirit stands ready for your cooperation and direction. The Holy Ghost wants to hold together with you.

V10 So I prophesied as he commanded me, and the breathe came into them, and they lived, and stood up on their feet, an exceeding great army.

What a leap: from very disjointed dry bones to an exceedingly great army! Ephesians 3:20 ***Now unto him that is able to do exceedingly abundantly above all that we ask or think, according to the power that works in us.***

When you are in the Spirit, and the word of God is rising from your spirit, your mouth and tongue become weaponised. You can pull down strongholds, obliterate generational curses and cast down the work of darkness. Out of the mouth of the babes and sucklings he has ordained strength. You can proclaim life to a struggling career, and there will be a breakthrough. You shall proclaim healing and the disease will have to go. No Compromise. Your tongue is the launching pad for missiles. Its not words only coming out of your mouth: its missiles! It is Holy Spirit inspired words. The Lord Jesus Christ said the words that he spoke were spirit and life. They are irresistible, indomitable and irreversible. Confess victory and you will possess victory. Proclaim healing and healing will be yours. We believe and thus we speak. We have the same spirit of faith. We believe and thus we speak, according to 2 Corinthians 4:13.

The Holy Spirit is also called an advocate.

Thank God the Spirit knows the mind of the Lord and he himself presents our case to the Lord in a more persuasive way than we can.

In my own personal walk with Christ I have found tongues to be indispensable.

I speak in tongues a lot but there are some special tongues which rise from the depth of my being when I confront an impossible or a particularly challenging situation. I ALWAYS GET MY VICTORY! Once when I was still in college I fell ill during the holiday. After a surgical operation I struggled to recover in time to get back to college. After seeking medical help from various quarters I was still no better three weeks into the new trimester. All medical options had been exhausted and time was running out. I needed to go back to college on time. The college was strict and had no qualms about failing you if you did not meet their standards regardless of your mitigating circumstances .The Holy Spirit stirred me to pray in special tongues. I had a note of victory. My Father was surprised to see my night gown robed and pyjama clad frail form dancing with much rapture! Smith Wigglesworth said the man who believes God will laugh when he sees the situation deteriorating.

We walk not by sight but by faith.

We have the same Spirit of Faith. We believe and thus we speak! I began to speak my healing. I began to callings things that be not as though they were. My healing came speedily after speaking thus in tongues and confessing positively.

And I was soon in college again.

There was only the other issue of exams and assignments since I had fallen behind. Isn't it heartening to know that the Lord does not do half measures? His very first act in intervening for you is his down payment, a pledge and a guarantee that he will meet you all the way. The Lord gave me a dream. I was playing soccer. I had the ball and was running towards the goal. As I got into 'the box' and before striking the ball, the goalkeeper screamed and ran away from the goal post. It was a walk over for me! Much to everyone's amazement, I passed with flying colours while others who had started the term on time struggled to pass.

Roberts Ludlum, author of God's Generals says he is a blessed man. He lives only four miles from Rhema and six miles from Oral Roberts University. Roberts, author of God's Generals reminisces about the times he would pass by a restaurant in Tulsa and would see Brother Hagin in the restaurant talking in tongues. Similarly Brother Hagin would pull next to him at the traffic light and Roberts would notice that KEH would be speaking in tongues. KEH liked to quote Paul's statement,

'I speak in tongues more than you all.'

Lets go back to *1 Corinthians 14:*

***13 Wherefore let him that speaketh in an unknown tongue, pray that he may interpret*.**

14 if I pray in an unknown tongue my spirit prayeth but my understanding is unfruitful.

15 What is it then? I will pray with the spirit and I will pray with the understanding also---

KEH points out that one doesn't have to interpret what one has said in tongues all the time but at times the spirit will give an interpretation of what you are praying for. That way one is able to pray with both the Spirit and with the understanding.

He had won many a victory by praying in tongues. Baptism in the Holy Ghost an initial experience. It is just the threshold to great things if one can press on in the things of God. He lamented the fact that a lot of Christians remained stuck in nostalgia about the day they were filled with the Holy Spirit. They never developed spiritually into the knowledge of the Holy Ghost, got into a closer walk with the Holy Spirit. The reason behind the stunted growth lay primarily in limited fellowship with the Holy Spirit. A Christian should be conscious of the mighty one inside him, who sees him to victory in every situation he encounters. As this consciousness takes root and becomes pervasive, the Holy Spirit becomes more and more real and one becomes saturated with the presence of the Holy Spirit.

In January 1963 KEH was ministering in a Full Gospel Church. One night as they waited upon the Lord, the Spirit of Prayer fell and everyone lay on the floor praying. More than an hour and a half later, the congregation had dispersed and it was just him and the Pastor. He noted that towards the end of the prayer session, while lost in the spirit he kept doing something peculiar. With his thumb and index finger he was tracing a circle inside those fingers.

'I would go all around that circle one way and then I'd come back around it, praying in tongues the whole time.'(Roberts 1988:33.)

He would go three quarters of the way round the circle and then come back round it. He would still be praying in tongues all the time.

'I'd go half way around it, then back again, still praying in tongues. I'd go a quarter of the way around, and trace it back again, praying in tongues' (Hagin 1988:33.)

He wondered what he was doing. Then the interpretation came,

'You are going in a circle in your ministry. You'll go all the way around that circle, and then go back around over it over and over again.' (Hagin 1988:34).

KEH noted that he was going round and round in circles. He was about to go back to the same church for the ninth time. Still interpreting the tongues the Lord told him to break out of the circle of holding meetings in church, stop holding meetings in churches. It thwarts church growth and also his ministry's growth. He was to use a neutral place because denominations were prejudiced against each other. He needed to make another circle. KEH found himself making a little larger circle with his finger. This second circle was putting his sermons into print. The third circle was putting his sermon on tapes. He was also to go on the radio and teach. Everyone on radio was preaching, but the Lord told him to TEACH. All these plans took off and worked with clock like precision!

Mighty miracles are either wrought or lost depending on our ability to sense God's burden and pray in the power of the Holy Ghost. When one senses the burden to pray, and yields to the Lord's bidding , he will allow the Holy Spirit to lay hold together with him, giving him the unction to 'pray out unknown situations according to the will of God.'

It is the spirit which knows the unknown dangers, opportunities, revivals, soul winning doors------.

'It seems that God is limited by our prayer lives, he can do nothing for humanity unless someone asks him to do it.' KEH would often quote John Wesley.

The Lord wants to work with us to shape future events. However the vehicle for that partnership is for us spending time in fellowship with the Lord. Praying in the power of the Holy Spirit. It is then that the breakthrough will come.

If the **clouds** be **full** of rain, they empty themselves upon the earth.

Ecclesiastics 11:3 tells us.

A lot of folks wonder why it seems like God does not talk to them. It is important to reiterate this. Saints just go on their knees pray in tongues a bit and walk away. No. Believers must be willing to pray in tongues at length, talking mysteries to the Lord. Then let the Lord talk back mysteries to them in the language they understand .And the Lord will use them.

One day I prayed in tongues for a very, very long time. After that I knew that something had shifted in the spiritual world. Some church members who had been pillars in my church and had stopped coming, miraculously resurfaced with renewed zeal.

Kenneth E Hagin's Prayer for the Church

In Tongues: Beyond the Upper Room, KEH laments the prayerlessness state of the church. The church, he noted had settled for a standard that was far below what the Lord longed for. The spiritual things have been relegated into the periphery and increasingly becoming less real while natural and physical things occupy the center ground and dominate the Saints. Our reasonable service to present ourselves as a living sacrifice to God is now being neglected as we pursue earthly things.

The Lord was the Father of the Spirits and supernaturally communicates with us in the spirit. The Saints however are not in direct contact with the Lord as they neglect Paul's statement 'If I pray in an unknown tongue, my spirit prayeth.' This powerful means of prayer lies neglected today and yet the Christian's power is waning. The Lord's will, his biddings and leadings are ignored. What the Lord wants to do for us, through us, with us and in us goes unattended. We are ill positioned. May the Lord keep moving us to a place where we are ready to receive from him.

The church through travail and intercession should give birth to the next wave of God's move. When we start responding to the Lord's bidding and catch the urgency of his message, we rise up in faith and in power. We become the Giants on earth as the Lord has always intended.

A REVIVAL IS COMING!

Kenneth E Hagin's prayer is echoed by his son Kenneth W Hagin. He notes that the last days are upon us and the Lord is calling for those who are willing to pay the price. He laments the fact that the body of Christ has stopped short at the door to the supernatural for too long a time. The church needs to walk through the door and begin to walk in the Spirit's power and revelation. Speaking in tongues was just the threshold, the start. As we avail ourselves to the Holy Ghost he will start to use us every day to bring about his purposes on planet earth.

1n 2018 while I was praying the Holy Spirit spoke to me clearly that there is a move of the Holy Ghost that is coming. We must pray for this revival. Charles Finney stated that where an event is foretold by prophecy the church must pray for the prophecy to be fulfilled. When Daniel read Jeremiah's scroll and realized theat the 70 years wait for Jerusalem will be restored was coming to an end, he got to his knees and began to pray. Jeremiah was a Prophet but he spent more time talking to God than talking to man!

Genesis 1

Higher Grounds and Boundless Possibilities.

generations to come. KEH evidently saw greater things on the horizon as evidenced by his prophetic utterances in To**ngues: Beyond the Upper Room**. Great miracles had been wrought at the hands of great man of faith, yes, but more exploits lie ahead. We have only been in the periphery. Great things do lie ahead of us. He said people should not live on the old wave of revival. A revival is coming. The next wave will be higher than both the healing revival and the charismatic revival. In fact the next wave will be higher than both revivals put together. The church needs to pray the revival through though. Few, are the ones who deny their flesh's demands and pray the revival through. Such a deep dimension is needed today or the depth will be lost to us and new generations

KEH noted how several decades ago, the Americans became concerned when the Russians were able to put the first Sputnik out in space. Billions of dollars were poured into the space race. However the early astronauts didn't go far. They only barely left the earth's atmosphere: they didn't know how to maneuver in Space. In some way, observes KEH, some of us have reached the 'edge of the Spirit Realm in prayer.' We however don't know how to maneuver out there and therefore the prayer warriors have to take it one step at a time. As we avail ourselves to the Lord, going deeper and deeper in praying in tongues, the Lord will lead us into a deeper realm of prayer where miracles and revelations abound. KEH confesses that he had been there a few times and it was a frightening experience. He thought he might not come back at times. Enoch went out so far in the spiritual realm he didn't come back-KEH observed.

When more and more saints pray, the manifestation of the presence of God, and the demonstration of the Holy Ghost will be commonplace! It will be the rule and not the exception. KEH exhorted the saints to spend more time, in the things of God. Other things maybe legitimate, but they must not get in the way of the things of the Spirit. We have been like children wading in water, at the edge of the body of water , saying O what a great experience we have had. There is a deeper experience to have. Many have only touched the realm of the spirit but have not been fully immersed in it. We need to go further than knee deep, loin deep and swim in the spirit as the Prophet Ezekiel did in the book of Ezekiel 47. There is a call to the body of Christ to wait upon the Lord. Flow in the gifts of the Holy Spirit. We need to deny the flesh, deny ourselves and spend time in prayer, seeking the face of the Lord and not be hindered by our own pursuits. Paul, in essence asked Timothy 'who being a soldier entangles himself with the affairs of the world?'

We need to avail ourselves to the things of the Spirit. The spiritual realm can become as real the natural realm to us if we communicate and commune with the Lord continually.

The next wave of the Spirit, sweeping a mighty harvest into the kingdom, depends on us giving birth to that wave through praying in the spirit. Standing in the gap, spending hours on end on our knees, interceding for the Lord to have his way is the Lord's call today. Then multitudes will be swept into the kingdom in a bumper harvest hitherto unseen!

References

Hagin KE (2007) *Tongues Beyond the Upper Room* Tulsa Faith Library Publications

Roberts O (1993) *Unleashing the Power of Praying in the Spirit* Tulsa Harrison House